CHAUCER

The Franklin's Tale

To
A.G.H. *and* H.H.H.

CHAUCER
The Franklin's Tale

---

edited by
PHYLLIS HODGSON

THE ATHLONE PRESS

Published by
THE ATHLONE PRESS
90–91 *Great Russell Street, London* WC1B 3PY
The Athlone Press is an imprint of
Bemrose UK Limited

© *Phyllis Hodgson* 1960, 1973

First edition 1960
Seventh impression, with new Bibliography, 1973
Eighth impression 1980

ISBN 0 485 61007 8

Printed in Great Britain by
WESTERN PRINTING SERVICES LTD
BRISTOL

CONTENTS

ACKNOWLEDGEMENTS

This book owes much to previous Chaucerian studies and to the advice of friends and colleagues. The editor is especially indebted to Dr E. Jaffé, Professor E. G. R. Taylor, Professor G. Tillotson, and Mr A. G. Dewey of the Athlone Press.

P. H.

A NOTE ON REFERENCES

Unless otherwise stated references to works of Chaucer other than *The Franklin's Tale* follow the text and the line and page numbering of *The Complete Works of Geoffrey Chaucer*, edited by F. N. Robinson, 2nd edn., Oxford University Press, London, 1957 (published in U.S.A. by Houghton Mifflin Co., Boston, Mass.).

The letters included in line references to *The Canterbury Tales* designate the commonly accepted groupings of the tales (see page 110).

INTRODUCTION

The Franklin's Tale has not hitherto been published separately in England. The omission is surprising. It might be claimed that this is the most gracious of all *The Canterbury Tales* with its glowing illustration of the virtues of generosity and of fidelity to a plighted word and its complete freedom from any rascality. The plot delights by its shapeliness, its maintained suspense, and by the twist at the end. The characters are all likeable, sensitively depicted, and subtly contrasted as they react to situations and to each other. Their experiences are unfolded with a consistent logic and with a variety in the telling of imaginative description, spirited dialogue, philosophical reflection, sentimental soliloquy, parody, humour, pathos and irony. Memorable scenes follow in quick succession —the initial marriage contract between Arveragus and Dorigen; Dorigen's fearful vigil by the shore in her husband's absence; the May festivities in the garden; the Squire Aurelius's declaration of his love for Dorigen and her imposition of a seemingly impossible task as the condition of her favour; Aurelius's hopeless abandonment to grief; his rescue by his brother; their meeting with the magician; their entertainment in the magician's house leading up to their bargaining for the achievement of the seemingly impossible task; the magician's performance; Aurelius's announcement to Dorigen of the fulfilment of her condition; Dorigen's dilemma; Dorigen's confession to her husband and his reaction; Dorigen's journey to keep her promise; Aurelius's compassion and generous renunciation; Aurelius's own dilemma; his final settlement with the magician.

This tale, moreover, warmed by Chaucer's sympathy

7

for his fellow-creatures and conditioned throughout by his astonishingly wide cultural interests, bears the unmistakable impress of the poet's individual genius in the full maturity of his art. It is provided with a setting unusually comprehensive even among *The Canterbury Tales*, for in the development of his plot Chaucer has not only drawn extensively upon his lively reading in contemporary French and Italian literature, Boethius's *De Consolatione Philosophiae*, and in the works of some of the Church Fathers, but he has also made masterly use of particulars of oceanic and geographical lore, astronomy, astrology, and the craft of magic.

Such wealth of learning naturally calls for detailed annotation, but no one should be deterred by the weight of editorial comment from reading a story which is highly enjoyable and fully intelligible in itself. Unfamiliar words and phrases are translated in the Glossary, baffling allusions explained in the Notes.

It cannot be pretended, however, that full understanding can be reached without further consideration of the significance of *The Franklin's Tale* in the wider context of *The Canterbury Tales*. For just appreciation, the tale must be read on several levels, with an awareness of perspective which includes the Franklin, wholly and intimately associable with his tale, and also Chaucer, the creator, who calls into being both the Franklin and the creatures of *The Franklin's Tale*.

When read in the light of the medieval cosmology in which Chaucer himself believed—for he knew no other (see Appendix IV)—the central story itself will have a meaning quite different from that which would be found by a modern reader knowing only the twentieth-century physics of the universe and taking for granted a heliocentric system insignificantly placed in the Milky Way, which itself is but one of unnumbered galaxies of stars wandering about in unmeasured space.

Introduction

Though it is true that the technical allusions are surprisingly few in a story which turns upon the control of natural forces by the Clerk's skill in astrological magic, and none of these in any way obscures the account of the fortunes and the changing relationships of Dorigen and her husband, Aurelius and the Clerk, yet a close examination of them is unexpectedly rewarding (see Appendix IV). Let no reader be daunted by the long, complicated and abstruse description of how the Clerk set about the feat of removing the rocks. The jargon of Alfonsine Tables, roots, centres, arguments, equations, proves to be ambiguous, and too vague to afford any precise information. It need not be understood by us since we can be sure that not only the majority of the Canterbury Pilgrims but also Chaucer's actual audience were out of their depth. Since there is no doubt from his *Astrolabe* and *The Equatorie of the Planetis* that Chaucer himself had mastered the subject, it seems evident that his purpose here was artistic rather than instructive. We can only guess at his motive. Possibly it was to throw further light on the Franklin, who had prefaced his long description of astrological processes by the assertion that he himself 'ne kan no termes of astrologye' and who might have been using jargon which he had picked up without understanding it, or giving a garbled selection of information out of his contemptuous disapproval of astrology as 'swich a supersticious cursednesse' (564). More likely it was meant to enhance the portrait of the Clerk and to lend an air of strangeness to the central event of the story. No matter how difficult the lines, their effect is clear. The magic is left mysterious, and the Franklin has established beyond doubt that this particular Clerk was very clever indeed. The inevitable conclusion is that the whole passage was intended to impress rather than inform, and is, in fact, the more impressive the less it is understood.

The study of the possible sources of *The Franklin's Tale*,

9

which forms the second part of this Introduction, will be
even more illuminating. Only by comparing Chaucer's
conceptions with their analogues can we realize the
amazing creativeness of his art.

THE FRANKLIN AND HIS TALE

In his *General Prologue to the Canterbury Tales* Chaucer in-
cluded the Franklin in his account of the 'nine and
twenty' men and women who assembled one April day
at the Tabard Inn in Southwark to ride on a pilgrimage
to the shrine of St Thomas of Canterbury and fell in with
the plan of their Host, who was to accompany them, that
each should tell four tales in competition for a free supper,
two on the outward and two on the homeward journey.
Chaucer died before his plan was fulfilled, when only
twenty-three tales were told and only a proportion of the
links between them supplied. Scholars are still disputing
the intended order of the existing tales (see Appendix I,
'The Canon of Chaucer's Works'), but by common agree-
ment they place *The Franklin's Tale* late in the series, at
the earliest after those of the Knight, Miller, Reeve, Wife
of Bath, Clerk, Merchant and Squire.

Like most of the personages introduced in the *General
Prologue* and first observed with the sweeping insight of
the omniscient narrator, the Franklin later gains in depth
and vitality both through the report of his words and
actions in the links between the tales and through the
appropriateness of the story which he himself contributes.

He is presented as a country gentleman, a wealthy
landowner, comfortably established at home and now
riding in the company of the important and outstanding
Sergeant of the Law. The impressive list of public offices
he had held—as president at the sessions of the Justices
of the Peace, as a member of parliament ('knight of the
shire'), as sheriff (an administrative office of the Crown
ranking in the shire next to that of lord lieutenant), and

as county auditor or possibly as pleader in court ('countour')—attests that he combined practical ability and industry with his Epicurean love of good living. His prodigious hospitality accorded with his worldly success and with his natural disposition, which Chaucer classified as 'sangwyn'.[1] The only anxiety he betrayed was on account of his son, who frequented low company rather than society where he might acquire culture and the manners common to men of good breeding. There is a strong hint that the Franklin, like Chaucer himself, belonged to that section of society middle-class by birth but sufficiently favoured, rich, and powerful to advance into the nobleman's way of life. Naturally the Franklin was class-conscious. The Knight and his son, his social superiors, were the story-tellers he most admired and imitated, and attention is drawn in the Notes to many resemblances in themes and style. His admiration for the accomplishments of the Squire expressed more eloquently than words his disappointment at his own son's failure to live up to the standard of conduct he expected of the nobility. The Franklin's preoccupation with the idea of 'gentillesse'[2] irritated the Host, who, town-bred himself, failed, perhaps, to recognize the social distinction of this country gentleman and was provoked to rudeness, to which the Franklin replied with good-humoured tact, while nevertheless persisting in his theme—an example of the geniality, practical common sense and perseverance which had brought him worldly success.

Here was the character especially suited by his temperament and dignity, his public-spiritedness, his experi-

---

[1] Cf. a fourteenth-century definition in *Secreta Secretorum*, ed. R. Steele, London, 1898, pp. 19f.: 'The sangyne by kynde sholde lowe Joye and laghynge, and company of women, and moche Slepen and syngynge—of good will and wythout malice—fre and lyberall, of fayre semblaunt.'

[2] See Notes, 46.

ence in jurisdiction and his acceptance of the everyday world to settle a controversy which had raged among the Pilgrims with increasing acrimony and to raise the tone of the company which, through a succession of lewd stories and intervening animosities, had fallen sharply from that set by the courtly elegance of the Knight's opening tale. From the start, mounting interest had been shown in relationships in love. The Knight had begun with an aristocratic tale of rivalry between equally matched courtly lovers, which the Miller had parodied on a lower social level, describing the rivalry between a worthless clerk and a squire, and adding cuckoldry to the theme. The Reeve had doubled the bawdry and the farce. The Wife of Bath had concentrated upon the work-ability of married life, preaching the domination of the wife as the essential condition of success. To this the Clerk had added a counterpoise by describing a tyran-nous husband's harsh domination over a wholly sub-servient wife, and by concluding his tale with ironical praise of the Wife of Bath. Following the Clerk, the Mer-chant, with more savage irony, had indicted the whole institution of matrimony in the story of a jealous old dotard knight fooled by his young bride, and the Squire, requested to 'sey somwhat of love' which would raise the prevailing tone, had become bogged in a shapeless and seemingly endless story of magic and desertion. It re-mained for the Franklin to resolve the argument and restore a sense of proportion by a story of ideal relations between a man and wife, based on a reconciliation be-tween the conventions of courtly love and the terms of a workable marriage, a marriage secure through the lack of jealousy and the renunciation of all domination in favour of mutual concessions and forbearance.[1] He clothed his plea for tolerance and good faith in human relationships in a tale generous and sensible like himself,

[1] See Notes, 53ff., 90.

without a knave or a fool, and in which men of different ranks, a Knight, a Squire, and a Clerk, vied with each other in magnanimity.

His literary interests are fully in keeping with what we have already learnt about him. Belonging to the country and not to the court, the Franklin is somewhat behind the times, and, unfamiliar with the latest fashions in narrative, he adopts the rather outmoded form of the Breton lay.[1] He is, however, acquainted with the literary conventions of courtly love,[2] but his practical common sense rejects what is extravagant and unsocial in rules of behaviour which, carried to their extreme, encouraged adultery. Thus Arveragus before his marriage and Aurelius before he learns wisdom are described as behaving in accordance with the tradition: both adore from afar a beautiful lady of noble kindred, both suffer torment and pain because they dare not speak their love, both are utterly subservient—Arveragus undertakes many a great enterprise for his lady's sake, Aurelius composes songs, passes sleepless nights in weeping, loses his appetite, pines and swoons. The Franklin retains the devotion and unselfishness of the courtly love relationship, but he also shows Arveragus's assumption of control after marriage and Aurelius's growing respect for the faithfulness of a wife. The Franklin is sufficiently interested in romance material to treat of magic, but so firmly orthodox in his faith as to declare that 'swich folye' is 'in oure dayes . . . nat worth a flye'.

The teller is in perfect accord with his tale. Chaucer seems deliberately to emphasize this by making the magician in some respects reflect the Franklin's own hospitality and insistence on a high standard of service. The portrait might perhaps have been drawn from life,[3]

[1] See Notes, 1–7.   [2] See Notes, 22–6, 90.

[3] See J. M. Manly, *Some New Light on Chaucer*, New York, 1926, pp. 162ff., and K. L. Wood-Legh, *Review of English Studies*, iv, pp. 145–51.

but one cannot help feeling that into this ample-minded and kindly country gentleman, who in fact is said to have held offices that Chaucer himself had occupied (see Appendix I, 'Chaucer's Life and Times'), the poet has projected his own fairness and wisdom, his opinion on matrimony, his own tolerant, half-humorous appraisal of life.

POSSIBLE SOURCES

Analogy and Originality in *The Franklin's Tale*

The Franklin's Tale differs from many of the other serious tales told by the Canterbury Pilgrims in that it is not largely drawn from any obvious literary source. Its plot of the consequences of a rash promise is that of a folk tale believed to have originated in the East. There are ancient parallels in Sanscrit, as well as in Burmese, Persian, Turkish, and Hebrew, of a lady's promise to a second lover which is given in a moment of embarrassment and later kept with the consent of her first and true love, with the result that the contagion of his generosity, or of her faithfulness, effects a remission of the debt; and to these the question is attached: Who was the noblest, or the most generous, of the three? A western group with a similar plot exists, with analogues in Spanish, French, Italian and English, ultimately derived from an Oriental version, but distinguished from it by the introduction of a magician. Within the western group *The Franklin's Tale* is closest to the story as told by the Italian writer, Boccaccio (1313–75), which occurs in the fourth narrative of the *questioni d'amore* episode which forms a small and insignificant piece of the long prose romance, *Il Filocolo*, and again in the *Decameron* as one of the stories of the tenth day. It will be shown later that *The Franklin's Tale* might well owe its plot, the general relationship of the characters and their readjustments to each other, together with various other features of the story, to Boccaccio's

14

works, but, if this is so, the Italian version has been almost completely disguised by the Franklin's description of his source as a Breton lay, by various accretions, and, most of all, by Chaucer's fresh conception of the characters and their reactions, his individual emphasis on certain values in the story, and his interpolation of themes which make *The Franklin's Tale* crucial in the drama of the pilgrimage which forms the framework of *The Canterbury Tales*.

In *Il Filocolo*, a queen and her companions discuss problems of love in a beautiful garden. Menedon tells the story here summarized:

A rich and noble knight was married to a most beautiful and noble lady (cf. *FT*, 22, 26–7), whom he deeply loved. Another knight, called Tarolfo, also loved this lady, for she was lovely and he desired nothing but her (cf. *FT*, 231). He tried to win her favour in many ways, often passing in front of her house, jousting, sending messages, promising great gifts, whereby she might know his intent. The lady perceived his purpose, but gave no answering sign, hoping that he would desist. But Tarolfo went on, following the precept of Ovid that dripping water will wear away hard stone. The lady was afraid that her husband might learn of these attentions and assume that she had encouraged Tarolfo, so she thought up a ruse to get rid of him. She sent a message to him, swearing by her gods and her good faith that she would be his love (cf. *FT*, 281–2, 289–90) if he would provide for her a large and beautiful garden in January, full of plants and flowers and trees and fruit. She said to herself that this was impossible (cf. *FT*, 293) and in this way she could shake him off. Tarolfo, understanding her motive and knowing her requirement to be impossible (cf. *FT*, 301), replied that he would not rest until he could give her what she asked. He left the country, wandered about, and finally came to Thessaly. On a miserable plain at the foot of the mountains, he encountered a wretched old fellow, bearded, undersized, very spare of person, in poor attire gathering herbs and roots. Tarolfo enquired what he was doing, and the old man, who said his name was Tebano, replied that he was gathering herbs for medicine. Tarolfo in turn told of his grief and of his hopeless undertaking.

Introduction

When asked what he would give to anyone who could provide the garden, he offered: 'Half my castles and treasures.' But when and how could it be done? Tebano asserted that it could be done whenever Tarolfo wished, and that he need not worry about how. Tarolfo was then almost as joyful as if he already held his lady in his arms (cf. *FT*, 528–30). He wished for no further delay (cf. *FT*, 524–5). Tebano threw away his herbs, collected his books and other gear (cf. *FT*, 565–70), and the two reached the desired city (cf. *FT*, 532–4) very near to the beginning of January (cf. *FT*, 535–6) in which month the garden was required. Tebano watched for an auspicious night (cf. *FT*, 554–5) and a full moon before beginning his enchantments. He appealed to Hecate who had helped him before in such tasks as producing streams and drying up seas; made a three-day journey in a dragon chariot to distant lands in Europe, Asia and Africa, to collect such ingredients as roots and herbs, stone, sand, lungs of venomous serpents, flesh of infamous witches, etc., and from these he concocted a magic brew, which he stirred with a dry olive twig. When the twig turned green and bore fruit, he poured the liquid over the chosen spot, which straightway blossomed and bore fruit. Then he returned to Tarolfo and said that he had done what he commanded, and all was according to his wish. The next day Tarolfo approached the lady at a great festivity in the city (cf. *FT*, 598–9) and informed her that after long labour he had provided what she had demanded, and that the garden was ready for her to see and enjoy at her pleasure (cf. *FT*, 625–7). The lady, greatly astonished (cf. *FT*, 631) and incredulous, asked to see it. With her companions she entered the garden and picked flowers whilst others tasted the fruit. Then she turned to Tarolfo and said: 'Assuredly, sir knight, you have earned my love, and I am ready to keep my promise.' But she begged him to wait until her husband was away hunting, or in another part of the city (cf. *FT*, 643), when, without fail, he should have his will. She returned to her own chamber full of grief, and wondering how she might keep her promise, but she could devise no reasonable excuse for returning to Tarolfo, which increased her care. Her husband many times asked her what was wrong (cf. *FT*, 753ff.), but she replied: 'Nothing.' Finally she broke down under re-

16

peated questioning, and told him all. The husband thought for a long time, but realizing her essential innocence, told her to keep her promise—but secretly (cf. *FT*, 773ff.). The lady protested that she would rather kill herself than bring dishonour on him (cf. *FT*, 649ff., *FT*, 891-2), or displease him. The husband reassured her that he would not be displeased, nor would he hold her any the less dear; she must be careful, however, not to make any more such promises (cf. *FT*, 833), even though the fulfilment seemed impossible. Decking herself, and with attendants (cf. *FT*, 779-80), the lady made her way to the lodging of Tarolfo, where she bashfully presented herself. Tarolfo left Tebano, with whom he was sitting, and full of wonder and joy received her with honour, enquiring the reason for her coming (cf. *FT*, 801-2). 'To be entirely at your pleasure. Do with me what you will', she said. Tarolfo imagined what scenes she must have had with her husband; whereupon the lady told him exactly what had happened. Hearing the truth, Tarolfo marvelled and pondered long. Realizing the generosity of her husband, he felt that anyone who wronged such a man would be worthy of the greatest shame. He praised the lady for faithfully bringing what was due to him. 'I account that I have received from you what I desired. Wherefore, when it may please you, you may return to your husband and thank him on my behalf for his kindness to me, and beg him to forgive me for the folly I have committed against him. I shall never consider such a thing again.' The lady thanked him for his great courtesy, and joyfully returned to her husband and told him all that had happened (cf. *FT*, 837-9). Tebano asked Tarolfo how the matter stood, and when he knew, asked if he were to lose all that had been promised. Tarolfo bade him take half his castles and treasure. To which Tebano responded: 'The gods forbid, since the knight was so generous and you no more churlish, that I should be less noble (cf. *FT*, 901-4). Above all things in the world I am pleased that I have served my turn, and I will take that in reward for my services.' And he would take none of Tarolfo's possessions.

When the company argued which of the three men had shown himself the most generous, the queen gave the final decision that the husband's generosity should be placed above that of Tarolfo and Tebano, since honour is more precious than either wealth or a lover's pleasure.

RESEMBLANCES TO IL FILOCOLO AND THE DECAMERON

The extract from *Il Filocolo* summarized above is the source most widely admitted for *The Franklin's Tale*. Close comparison with the original Italian will reveal almost no verbal similarity, and only a few significant correspondences in detail—viz. an impossible task imposed by a lady as the price of her love—which among the analogues occurs only in Boccaccio; the choice of early January for the date of the miracle; a magician who watches the moon and waits for an auspicious time. Possibly Chaucer was drawing upon his memory of Boccaccio's story for the shape of his plot. If this is so, he freely refurbished the story, and transferred and transformed particulars. The unnaturalness of a garden as beautiful in January as in May might well have suggested the contrast between the appearance of the garden when Dorigen played there with her friends in May:

> Which May hadde peynted with his softe shoures
> This gardyn ful of leves and of floures.   (199–200)

and in January when Dorigen made her way thither in bleakness of spirit:

> The bittre frostes with the sleet and reyn
> Destroyed hath the grene in every yerd.   (542–3)

Arveragus's somewhat unexpected reception of his wife's confession—'with glad chiere, in freendly wyse' (759)—may contain more than reassurance to someone in distress, and might reflect some of the Italian husband's relief on perceiving his wife's innocence. The rather harsh and unnecessary admonition to the Italian wife to make no more such promises has become a playful general warning from the Franklin:

> But every wyf be war of hire biheeste!   (833)

Some changes are obviously made to suit the wider context of *The Canterbury Tales*. Chaucer credits the long service of Tarolfo to Arveragus himself (22–5) for he is developing the theme of a workable marriage. He intensifies Dorigen's desperate plight by keeping Arveragus out of town for three days, whereas the Italian lady was anxiously waiting for her husband's absence. The single protest of the Italian wife that she would rather kill herself than bring dishonour on her husband is prolonged into a hundred lines of soliloquy spoken by Dorigen, appropriate enough to her desperate loneliness but really pointed by the Franklin at the Wife of Bath.

Boccaccio repeated the same story in the *Decameron* (Day 10, Story 5), in the novel of Gilberto, Ansaldo and Dianora, which Chaucer may also have seen, for some details in *The Franklin's Tale* are more reminiscent of this novel than of the account in *Il Filocolo*. Aurelius promised the magician £1000, cf. *Decameron*: 'a very great sum of money'. He exhorted Dorigen to remember her solemn promise:

> 'Ye woot right wel what ye bihighten me
> And in myn hand youre trouthe plighten ye . . .
> . . . have youre biheste in mynde . . .'   (619–27)

Compare Ansaldo's remark to Dianora: 'now remember the promise you made me and sealed with an oath'. Dorigen set out to keep her vow with a squire and a maid, Dianora, 'together with two of her friends and followed by her maid'. Aurelius's first reaction when he met Dorigen was compassion:

> And in his herte hadde greet compassioun
> Of hire and of hire lamentacioun,
> And of Arveragus . . .   (807–9)

Whereas Tarolfo was overwhelmed with admiration for the husband, Ansaldo's reactions also contained pity: 'his ardour began to give way to compassion'. A combination of these two, or even more, accounts is highly probable. Such conflation produced the description of the garden, for which the sources must be sought in *Il Filocolo* both in the garden in which the story was told, and in the garden produced by magic; in the garden of Boccaccio's *Teseida*; in Machaut's *Dit Dou Vergier*; and in descriptions of countless other gardens all related to the garden in the *Roman de la Rose*, and ultimately derived from the 'ideal landscape' described in treatises on rhetoric.[1]

DIFFERENCES FROM IL FILOCOLO AND THE DECAMERON

Remove all the passages for which the direct influence of Boccaccio may be claimed: most of *The Franklin's Tale* still remains—the personalities, the Breton and French scenes, the unique conditions of Arveragus's marriage, his long absence when Dorigen walked by the shore sighing for his return and weighing the problem of evil, the direct confession of Aurelius's love in the garden, the particular miracle required, the removal of the rocks, Aurelius's sickness and his brother's sympathy, the entertainment at the Clerk's house, the astrological magic, the complaint of Dorigen to Fortune, the financial quandary of Aurelius.

Characterization

Arveragus, Dorigen and Aurelius are different people from the nameless knight and lady, and Tarolfo in *Il Filocolo*, or again from Gilberto, Dianora and Ansaldo in the *Decameron*. The character of Arveragus is the least developed, but Chaucer adds to the account of his great love, which Boccaccio supplied, a report of his wooing, his warfaring, his letter-writing, and his social accomplishments. Unlike Boccaccio's knight, he shows no trace of jealousy. He is human, however, in his conflict of

[1] See Notes, 200ff.

feelings when he learns of his wife's plight. He first re-
assures her by kindness (759). As he determines upon the
only course to follow he realizes the chance of a gamble
on his rival's generosity (765) but also the possible conse-
quences of his decision, which make him 'brest anon to
wepe'. Throughout, his foremost thought is for his repu-
tation (773-5, 43-4).

Whereas Boccaccio makes little distinction between the
husband and the lover, Chaucer depicts Arveragus as a
shrewd, balanced, and mature man of action, in striking
contrast with the younger, more impulsive, extrava-
gantly passionate and sentimental Aurelius. In his colour-
ful appearance, his social accomplishments, his poetic
gifts, his behaviour in love, Aurelius belongs to a type[1]
ultimately descended from the ideal lover in the *Roman
de la Rose*. He may even have been directly inspired by the
Arcita of the *Teseida*, for Arcita also has to content
himself with merely looking on Emilia's face, as she is
unaware of his love (iv. 52-4, 62; cf. *FT*, 249-51), reso-
lutely conceals his passion (iv. 60-1; cf. *FT*, 228-35), and
takes part in the gay life of the court where he enjoys
great popularity (iv. 62; cf. *FT*, 221-6), giving utterance
to his complaints only in solitude (iv. 63-8; cf. *FT*,
235-40). Aurelius, however, comes to life before us
through the minute description of his every feeling and
reaction as he ranges through languishment and resolu-
tion, grief and despair, hope and relaxation, impatience,
timidity, joy, compassion, generosity, embarrassment,
relief. He is convincing as an individual when he naïvely
but ingeniously bargains with Apollo, relies implicitly
upon his elder brother, impulsively accepts the Clerk's
price though it is twice as much as he can afford and,
finding relief in hope, sleeps peacefully after the bargain,
loiters near Dorigen's house and contrives to meet her as
if by chance, impulsively releases her from her promise

[1] See Notes, 218.

when he sees her distress, repents of his reckless bargain, yet resolves to try to pay his debt in full. Aurelius no less than Arveragus gains our interest and respect far more than the husband and the lover in Boccaccio's tales.

Dorigen resembles her counterpart only in her noble birth and beauty. Boccaccio's heroine is a sophisticated lady of society, afraid of her husband's jealousy if she does not rid herself of the attentions of Tarolfo, of whose love she has long been aware. She is pleased with her ruse for shaking him off, and herself takes the initiative in offering him the impossible terms as the price of her love. When the garden appears, she keeps her presence of mind, asks to see it, and walks about in it with her friends, picking flowers. Part of her subsequent anxiety about her rash promise is her fear that she might find no excuse for escaping from her husband to keep it. Only after long questioning will she reveal the cause of her sorrow. When she is reassured by her husband and bidden to fulfil her vow, she remembers to adorn herself first. Dorigen is far more single-minded. Chaucer devotes more than two hundred lines to her reactions and reflections, but these are all centred in her husband—grief at his absence, anxiety for his safety, determination to be his 'humble trewe wyf'. She lives only for Arveragus. She is completely taken by surprise by Aurelius's avowal of love, which she rebuffs firmly and scornfully—and it would have been finally, if her natural kindness of heart had not led her to try to soften the blow by her playful afterthought intended only to persuade Aurelius of the impossibility of achieving her love. She knows nothing of astrological magic, and is so shattered by the news of the removal of the rocks that she has no heart to go and see for herself, but 'In al hir face nas a drope of blood'

> And hoom she goth a sorweful creature;
> For verray feere unnethe may she go.   (638–9)

After her three days' distraught resolution to kill herself,

Arveragus returns home and at once she pours out every-
thing. When her lover, meeting her in a busy street, asks
her where she is going, she answers, 'half as she were mad':

> 'Unto the gardyn, as myn housbonde bad,
> My trouthe for to holde, allas! allas!'   (803–5)

Dorigen could have been very dull if delineated by a
lesser master than Chaucer, but through his skill she
wins far more of our sympathetic regard than the Italian
lady. Our interest is aroused from the start in what will
happen to a typical lady of the romance world of courtly
love who takes a husband to be 'hir servant and hir lord'.
It soon appears that he has become her world and the
centre of all her thoughts, and that she is inconsolable in
his absence. A walk by the sea instead of delighting her
only increases her anguish:

> . . . 'Allas!' seith she,
> 'Is ther no shipe, of so manye as I se,
> Wol bryngen hom my lord?'   (145–7)

> But whan she saugh the grisly rokkes blake,
> For verray feere so wolde hir herte quake
> That on hire feet she myghte hire noght sustene.
>
> (151–3)

> 'But wolde God that alle thise rokkes blake
> Were sonken into helle for his sake!'   (183–4)

'Thise grisly feendly rokkes blake' which menace her
husband's return become indeed such an obsession that
naturally the most impossible task she can conceive to
shake off Aurelius is to

> '. . . remoeve alle the rokkes, stoon by stoon,
> That they ne lette shipe ne boot to goon.'
>
> (285–6)

When at the end she contemplates killing herself and,
with the tedious repetition of one distraught, strings
together a seemingly endless list of noble wives and
maidens who have preferred death to dishonour—all

taken from St Jerome's *Adversus Jovinianum* and including some not really relevant—one realizes that all she needs is her husband to give her counsel. She obeys his command as docilely as any Griselda. There is no doubt how this marriage has turned out, and who is 'in lordshipe above'.

The most subtly portrayed character in *The Franklin's Tale* is the nameless Clerk, who owes nothing to the wretched old Tebano, a creation inspired by classical sources. We first assume that he too had been a lively young student at the university of Orleans, eagerly studying natural magic 'al were he ther to lerne another craft' (419). This and many other details might easily have been drawn from life. When he actually appears on the scene he is still young, and his clandestine studies have stood him in good stead for he can anticipate the arrival of Aurelius and his brother and, meeting them on the way, astound them by showing them that he already knows the cause of their coming. His worldly prosperity increases their confidence in him—

> So wel arrayed hous as ther was oon
> Aurelius in his lyf saugh nevere noon. (479–80)

He demonstrates his skill before they dine by evoking illusions particularly suited to the young Squire—of hunting, hawking, jousting, and the greatest delight of all,

> . . . he hym shewed his lady on a daunce,
> On which hymself he daunced, as hym thoughte. (492–3)

But this he quickly dismisses, to whet Aurelius's appetite still more. After supper, when their spirits are mellowed, he shows his business capacity for hard bargaining, with an unexpected show of imperiousness and aloofness—

> He made it straunge, and swoor, so God hym save,
> Lasse than a thousand pound he wolde nat have. (515–16)

—a bargain which Aurelius, by now completely in his

power, cannot refuse. This Clerk, however, is no charlatan, and Chaucer takes pains to impress upon us his erudition and proficiency through which, by astrological magic, he makes the rocks disappear. He sharply and sternly interrogates Aurelius when he can pay only half his debt, but he is quickly stirred by the nobility of Arveragus, the anguish of Dorigen, and most of all the generosity of Aurelius. Though he can strike a hard bargain, he will uphold the dignity of his calling, and emulate the Knight and the Squire in magnanimity. With a wry joke he remits Aurelius's debt; his parody of Aurelius's earlier remission of Dorigen's debt reflects his own humorous acceptance of the irony of the situation.

There is no hint in Boccaccio's story of the sympathetic brother, a man of action and practical suggestions, who sentimentally cherishes happy memories of his college days and who weeps for the death of his old friends.

Signification

Such acute characterization coupled with serious reflections on life makes *The Franklin's Tale* more meaningful than the story in either *Il Filocolo* or the *Decameron*. Though Boccaccio, like Chaucer, weighted his narrative with the conviction of the infectious influence of generosity, the fortunes of his four people remain firmly fixed in the context of a problem of love, whereas Chaucer explicitly considered the same situations against the background of a successful marriage, based on tolerance and mutual give-and-take, without any domination, jealousy, or disloyalty. He developed the theme of happy wedded life at length in the beginning (34–97), and turned to it again towards the end (831–2, 843–8). Such a marriage must rest upon good faith, and Chaucer underlined more strongly than Boccaccio the paramount obligation of a solemn promise:

Trouthe is the hyeste thyng that man may kepe.　(771)

Introduction

Implicitly, throughout the story, Chaucer was illustrating the irony of fate. The original plot which contrasted the expectation of three people with its attainment held an element of irony which Chaucer intensified until it became all-pervasive. Thus Dorigen sincerely wishing to free herself from the attentions of Aurelius and by the very conditions she imposes giving effective proof that she is entirely devoted to her husband, thereby puts herself in Aurelius's power and gives him the right to claim her love. The rocks which once presented the greatest menace to the reunion of man and wife, when removed, nearly lead to their separation, and they vanish according to Dorigen's bidding long after she has ceased to care, or even to think, about them. This lady who in the beginning has accepted the promise of her future husband that he will 'hire obeye, and folwe hir wyl in al', in the end meekly and unprotestingly follows his command and relies wholly upon him. These ironic reversals, and the similar twists in the fortunes of Aurelius and the Clerk, induce a certain seriousness in the reader, though it must be admitted that there are few lines that explicitly prompt such an attitude. Chaucer only once strikes a profound and solemn note—when Dorigen ponders on the mystery of evil. There, in phraseology partly reminiscent of passages in Boethius's *De Consolatione Philosophiae* and possibly of the *Teseida*,[1] she wonders why a wise and beneficent God, who has shown His 'greet chiertee' in making man in His own image, could also create 'thise grisly feendly rokkes blake':

> '. . . how thanne may it bee
> That ye swiche meenes make it to destroyen,
> Whiche meenes do no good, but evere anoyen?' (174–6)

Elsewhere there is no comment—only the hint of the poet's own view of life reflected in the wry smile one

[1] See Notes, 157–85.

26

imagines on the lips of the Clerk as he takes his horse and
goes on his way.

OTHER POSSIBLE INFLUENCES

British Tradition

The other suggestions of possible indebtedness are incon-
clusive and controversial. Chaucer probably drew his
proper names from some Chronicle of British kings. The
names Arveragus and Aurelius both appear in Geoffrey
of Monmouth's *Historia Regum Britanniae*:

- IV. 15 Arviragus loved his wife Genuissa [the form of the
name might be connected with Dorigen] above all
things.
- VIII. 10 Aurelius sent for Merlin to remove by magic the
Giants' Dance from Ireland to Stonehenge.

In Layamon's *Brut*, 9808–55, Arviragus and his wife
Genuissa are associated with both the theme of a happy
marriage and also that of loyalty to a pledge. In this
poem the love of Genuissa for her lord is more stressed
than his for her:

> . . . cleopede to hire lauerde
> The leof hire wes on heorte.   (9812–13)

In 9816–19, 9846–7, 9854–5, she exhorts him on the
virtue and kingliness of keeping one's plighted word:
'Thu most holde that thu aer bihaehtest'. The names
and associations are so far the same, but there is little
else.

Contemporary life

Legends of how Merlin brought great stones by magic
from Ireland to Stonehenge might have given Chaucer
his first inspiration for the task of the removal of the rocks
in *The Franklin's Tale*, but the illusions produced by his
Clerk were the common stock of many medieval tales.[1]

[1] See Notes, 431ff.

The congruity of the Clerk's performance to the Squire's own world is surely due to Chaucer alone. The marvels recalled by the brother might well have been described from the poet's own living experience.[1] It may even be that his vivid portrayal of the Clerk was also from life. Orleans was noted for its gathering of astrologers in the fourteenth century, and Chaucer's friend, Deschamps, had been a student of law there, and had dabbled in astrology. Colin 'tregetour', possibly introduced by Chaucer in his *House of Fame* (1277–81), was practising his art at Orleans very near the time of the composition of *The Canterbury Tales* and was described in a French manual written in 1396 as 'un Englois qu'estoit fort nigromancien—qui savoit faire beaucoup des mervailles par voie de nigromancie'.[2]

Breton lays

The British names and the Breton topography prevent an easy rejection of the Franklin's description of his source as a Breton lay.[3] A Droguen, or Dorigien, was indeed the wife of Alain I of Brittany. Arveragus's house was 'nat fer fro Pedmark', probably Penmarc'h Point, where the shore at low tide still consists of great expanses of low reef and a fearful chain of granite rocks stretches some distance out to sea.[4] This was a place with literary associations; from here the dying Tristan looked longingly for the white sails of Iseault of Ireland, and a passage in a Tristan romance (such as in the thirteenth-century prose *Tristan*) might have suggested the watching of Dorigen by the shore. Nothing could be more characteristic of the coast of Brittany than 'thise grisly rokkes blake'.

Yet apart from the Franklin's introduction (1–5) little in the tale closely resembles any extant lay. Some of the same motifs do occur (e.g. the rash promise and faithful-

---

[1] See Notes, 431ff.   [2] Quoted from Robinson, p. 785.
[3] See Notes, 1–7.   [4] See Notes, 93, 100.

ness to it in *Sir Tristrem* and *Sir Orfeo*; the impossible conditions imposed in *Doon, Les Dous Amanz*; a lover's despair and a lady's passionate avowal of love in a garden in *Lanval*; a hero's parting from a grieving wife for warfare in England in *Eliduc*; the incompatibility of love and sovereignty in *Equitan*; the introduction of magic everywhere); but the development and the tone are quite different.

In view of Chaucer's usual accuracy in mentioning his sources, the possibility cannot be dismissed of a lost lay, which might even have been a common source for both Boccaccio's versions and *The Franklin's Tale*. The case against this rests merely on deduction, and deduction can never yield final proof, however arresting the arguments. Professor Tatlock has demonstrated the paradox that the setting of the tale, the real Brittany, is too exact for the setting of a Breton lay.[1] Moreover, the ancient colouring in the name 'Armorica' and in the reference to the pagan temple of 'Delphos', by which Chaucer made plausible the magic practices which 'hethen folk useden in thilke dayes—in oure dayes nat worth a flye', has no parallel in any of the extant lays. Magic, accepted with wonder as natural in the lays, has become an evil, which produces only illusions. The astrological additions are Chaucer's own. The moral strain of *The Franklin's Tale* is alien to the true lay.

Most convincing of all the arguments against a Breton lay source is an explanation of the Franklin's prologue which excludes an intent to mislead. It must be remembered that even today, after generations of scholarly investigators, little is certain about the origin and scope of the Breton lays, and much less would be known in the second half of the fourteenth century, when the type was long out of fashion in France, as it had become in England

[1] J. S. P. Tatlock, *The Scene of the Franklin's Tale Visited*, London, 1914.

before Chaucer's work revived an interest in it. There is some evidence that Chaucer had read the Auchinleck MS which contained two of the earlier English imitations of the lays, *Sir Orfeo* and the *Lay le Freyne*. It would seem the result of a deliberate paraphrasing of their introduction rather than coincidence that *The Franklin's Tale*, 1–5, contains exactly the same ideas as the introduction to the *Lay le Freyne* and also the same vagueness. When Chaucer wished to achieve diversity in the manner of *The Canterbury Tales*, why should he not include one in the short narrative form and with the generalized characterization of the Breton lay type? His story bore some striking resemblances to that of *Sir Orfeo* in its account of a happily wedded and devoted couple, grief at separation, faithfulness to a promise, magic hunts and hawking. Though the plot might have been taken from Boccaccio, Chaucer gave it a Breton dress to substantiate his introduction, and by an imaginative stroke of rare genius transmuted the miracle of a garden in January, which might have been situated anywhere, to the magical removal of rocks which were localized in Brittany.

CONCLUSION

Focusing thus on the characters in the foreground and on Chaucer's inventiveness, this discussion of indebtedness has clearly indicated—if the suggestions of source material are accepted—that *The Franklin's Tale* is at the most only a very free adaptation and a composite. This indication will be strengthened and also explained by a brief return to one of the underlying purposes of the Franklin's story, which it will be remembered is to settle the controversy about the possibility and the terms of a workable marriage and to restore among the company a sense of propriety. The numerous references in the Notes will supply the evidence for the following observations. The Franklin's long introduction is undoubtedly prompted by the Wife of Bath's preamble and tale, by the Clerk's tale and epilogue, and by the Merchant's tale: there are too many deliberate verbal echoes for it to be otherwise. The long list of virtuous maidens and chaste wives faithful to their first husbands is surely pointed at the Wife of Bath, who has argued learnedly, ingeniously, and at undue length, against virginity and in favour of multiple marriage. It was part of Chaucer's private joke to take the Franklin's examples from St Jerome's *Adversus Jovinianum*, a favourite treatise with the Wife's fifth husband, which she quoted herself but still remembered as a source of unbearable annoyance. The reiterated *gentil* and the exposition of *gentillesse* in the threefold climax of generosity are not only complementary to the Wife's groping definitions in her tale but also a dignified retort to the Host, who has rudely interrupted the Franklin's open admiration of this quality in the Squire. Possibly the Franklin has been most deeply offended by the savage bitterness of the Merchant's narrative, and to redress the impression left by that he takes the same pattern for his story—the relationships between the same social types, a knight, his wife, a squire—and the same setting of a beautiful garden; but with a faithful wife to replace the unfaithful one, and with the scene of illicit love and adultery adopted as a setting for the fruitless declaration of unlawful passion and as the tryst for the promise which is never to be fulfilled.[1] The types of knight and squire, ridiculed and vilified in *The Merchant's Tale*, shall be depicted again, this time on the model of the noble examples on the pilgrimage. The impression left by the clerk and the squire who practised knavery in *The Miller's Tale* shall be superseded by that of another pair who have both earned their rewards yet vie with each other in generous renunciation.

All such evidence points inevitably to one conclusion:

[1] See Notes, 95–7.

the Franklin's story was composed especially for him, and was intended by Chaucer for one particular stage in the drama of the pilgrimage. The chief inspiration for *The Franklin's Tale* is to be sought in what had preceded in it *The Canterbury Tales.*

A NOTE ON THE TEXT

The text of this edition, including the extract from the *General Prologue* and the Link to *The Franklin's Tale*, has been transcribed from the facsimile of the Ellesmere Manuscript (Manchester University Press, 1911). This manuscript, carefully written and elaborately decorated, is named after its former owner, Lord Ellesmere.

After careful consideration of the complete sets of variant readings in the other manuscripts, published by J. M. Manly and E. Rickert, *The Text of the Canterbury Tales* (Chicago, 1940), it was decided that the present edition, unlike its predecessors, should keep entirely to the Ellesmere text, wherever that is intelligible and not demonstrably wrong. Manly and Rickert produced evidence to show that it is practically impossible to reproduce the author's original text from the extant manuscripts. The relationship of some eighty manuscripts of *The Franklin's Tale* is particularly involved, not only because of alterations of wording and arrangement made by early scribes, but also because Chaucer himself was still revising, changing, and correcting, when copies of his earlier versions were already in circulation.

Manly and Rickert established for this tale twelve independent lines of transmission from Chaucer's original text. They found the following manuscripts to be of chief importance:

Ellesmere MS (El), written 1400–10. Henry E. Huntington Library, California.

Hengwrt MS (Hg), written 1400–10, probably by the same scribe as El, but from a different exemplar, or copy. National Library of Wales, Aberystwyth.

MS Gg iv. 27 (Gg), written 1420–40. University Library, Cambridge.

Rawlinson MS 223 (Ra³), written 1450. Bodleian Library, Oxford.

The Ellesmere text contains readings, sometimes a whole line

A Note on the Text

or more, not in any other manuscript and known technically as unique readings. Some of these are editorial changes that could have been made either by Chaucer himself, or by an intelligent scribe; others are more obviously suspect. However, since El is the only representative of one line of transmission, emendation (the alteration of its text to some other reading) must be a matter for subjective judgment with no certainty, and the less emendation, therefore, the better. Notice has been taken nevertheless of Manly and Rickert's warning that in every reading the Ellesmere text need not be that of most authority. Though it was clearly intended to be definitive, its unique readings must be carefully scrutinized. And so, where Hg differs significantly from El, and has the support of some of the other important manuscripts, its variants are given in the footnotes. Some of the outstanding textual problems of El are discussed in the Notes.

In transcribing from the Ellesmere manuscript, some changes have been made. Abbreviations have been expanded, and modern paragraphing, punctuation, and capitalization added. The spelling of the original has been retained, with these exceptions: þ is written *th*; ȝ is written *y*; *i/j, u/v* are distinguished according to modern usage; *ff* is written *F*. þ̄ appears as *þe*.

The Franklin's Tale

preceded by Chaucer's description of the Franklin in the General
Prologue *to* The Canterbury Tales *and the lines which link*
The Franklin's Tale *to* The Squire's Tale—*which it
follows.*

The Franklin, after the illustration in the Ellesmere MS. This manuscript, which was probably written about the time of Chaucer's death, contains portraits of all the Canterbury Pilgrims, including the poet himself.

The Franklin

[General Prologue, A 331–60]

A Frankeleyn was in his compaignye.
Whit was his heed, as is a dayesye;
Of his complexioun he was sangwyn.
Wel loved he by the morwe a sope in wyn;
To lyven in delit was evere his wone;
For he was Epicurus owene sone
That heeld opinioun that pleyn delit
Was verray felicitee parfit.
An housholdere, and that a greet, was he;
Seint Julian was he in his contree.   [340]
His breed, his ale, was alweys after oon;
A bettre envyned man was nevere noon;
Withoute bake mete was nevere his hous
Of fissh and flessh, and that so plentevous,
It snewed in his hous of mete and drynke,
Of alle deyntees that men koude thynke.
After the sondry sesons of the yeer,
So chaunged he his mete and his soper.
Ful many a fat partrich hadde he in muwe,
And many a breem and many a luce in stuwe.   [350]
Wo was his cook but if his sauce were
Poynaunt and sharpe, and redy al his geere.
His table dormant in his halle alway
Stood redy covered al the longe day.
At sessiouns ther was he lord and sire;

332 berd (El *alone has* heed).   340 he was.

37

Ful ofte tyme he was knyght of the shire;
An anlaas, and a gipser al of silk
Heeng at his girdel, whit as morne milk.
A shirreve hadde he been, and countour.
Was nowher swich a worthy vavasour.   [360]

The words of the Franklin to the Squire and the words of the Host to the Franklin

[Link, F 673–708]

'In feith, Squier, thow hast thee wel yquit
And gentilly. I preise wel thy wit,'
Quod the Frankeleyn, 'considerynge thy yowthe,
So feelyngly thou spekest, sire, I allowe the!
As to my doom, ther is noon that is heere
Of eloquence that shal be thy peere,
If that thou lyve; God yeve thee good chaunce,
And in vertu sende thee continuaunce!   [680]
For of thy speche I have greet deyntee.
I have a sone, and by the Trinitee,
I hadde levere than twenty pound worth lond,
Though it right now were fallen in myn hond,
He were a man of swich discrecioun
As that ye been! Fy on possessioun,
But if a man be vertuous withal!
I have my sone snybbed, and yet shal,
For he to vertu listeth nat entende;
But for to pleye at dees, and to despende   [690]
And lese al that he hath, is his usage.
And he hath levere talken with a page

689 listneth El.

Than to comune with any gentil wight
Where he myghte lerne gentillesse aright.'
    'Straw for youre gentillesse!' quod oure Hoost.
'What, Frankeleyn! pardee, sire, wel thou woost
That ech of yow moot tellen atte leste
A tale or two, or breken his biheste.'
    'That knowe I wel, sire,' quod the Frankeleyn.
'I prey yow, haveth me nat in desdeyn,   [700]
Though to this man I speke a word or two.'
    'Telle on thy tale withouten wordes mo.'
    'Gladly, sire Hoost,' quod he, 'I wole obeye
Unto youre wyl; now herkneth what I seye.
I wol yow nat contrarien in no wyse
As fer as that my wittes wol suffyse.
I prey to God that it may plesen yow;
Thanne woot I wel that it is good ynow.'

The Franklin's Tale

Thise olde gentil Britouns in hir dayes
Of diverse aventures maden layes,
Rymeyed in hir firste Briton tonge;
Whiche layes with hir instrumentz they songe,
Or elles redden hem for hir plesaunce.
And oon of hem have I in remembraunce,
Which I shal seyn with good wyl as I kan.
   But, sires, bycause I am a burel man,
At my bigynnyng first I yow biseche,
Have me excused of my rude speche.   10
I lerned nevere Rethorik, certeyn;
Thyng that I speke, it moot be bare and pleyn.
I sleepe nevere on the Mount of Pernaso,
Ne lerned Marcus Tullius Scithero.
Colours ne knowe I none, withouten drede,
But swiche colours as growen in the mede,
Or elles swiche as men dye or peynte.
Colours of Rethoryk been to queynte;
My spirit feeleth noght of swich mateere.
But if yow list, my tale shul ye heere.   20

   In Armorik, that called is Britayne,
Ther was a knyght that loved & dide his payne
To serve a lady in his beste wise;
And many a labour, many a greet emprise
He for his lady wroghte, er she were wonne.

For she was oon the faireste under sonne,
And eek therto comen of so heigh kynrede
That wel unnethes dorste this knyght, for drede,
Telle hire his wo, his peyne, and his distresse.
But atte laste she, for his worthynesse,   30
And namely for his meke obeysaunce,
Hath swich a pitee caught of his penaunce
That pryvely she fil of his accord
To take hym for hir housbonde and hir lord,
Of swich lordshipe as men han over hir wyves.
And for to lede the moore in blisse hir lyves,
Of his free wyl he swoor hire as a knyght
That nevere in al his lyf he, day ne nyght,
Ne sholde upon hym take no maistrie
Agayn hir wyl, ne kithe hire jalousie,   40
But hire obeye, and folwe hir wyl in al,
As any lovere to his lady shal,
Save that the name of soveraynetee,
That wolde he have for shame of his degree.

   She thanked hym, and with ful greet humblesse
She seyde: 'Sire, sith of youre gentillesse
Ye profre me to have so large a reyne,
Ne wolde nevere God bitwixe us tweyne
As in my gilt, were outher werre or stryf.
Sire, I wol be youre humble trewe wyf,   50
Have heer my trouthe, til that myn herte breste.'
Thus been they bothe in quiete and in reste.

   For o thyng, sires, saufly dar I seye,
That freendes everych oother moot obeye,
If they wol longe holden compaignye.
Love wol nat been constreyned by maistrye.
Whan maistrie comth, the god of love anon
Beteth hise wynges, and farewel, he is gon!

Love is a thyng as any spirit free.
Wommen, of kynde, desiren libertee,   60
And nat to been constreyned as a thral;
And so doon men, if I sooth seyen shal.
Looke who that is moost pacient in love,
He is at his avanta[g]e al above.
Pacience is an heigh vertu, certeyn,
For it venquysseth, as thise clerkes seyn,
Thynges that rigour sholde nevere atteyne.
For every word men may nat chide or pleyne.
Lerneth to suffre, or elles, so moot I goon,
Ye shul it lerne, wher-so ye wole or noon;   70
For in this world, certein, ther no wight is
That he ne dooth or seith somtyme amys.
Ire, siknesse, or constellacioun,
Wyn, wo, or chaugnynge of complexioun,
Causeth ful ofte to doon amys or speken.
On every wrong a man may nat be wreken.
After the tyme moste be temperaunce
To every wight that kan on governaunce.
And therfore hath this wise, worthy knyght,
To lyve in ese, suffrance hire bihight,   80
And she to hym ful wisly gan to swere
That nevere sholde ther be defaute in here.
    Heere may men seen an humble, wys accord.
Thus hath she take hir servant and hir lord,
Servant in love, and lord in mariage.
Thanne was he bothe in lordshipe and servage.
Servage? Nay, but in lordshipe above,
Sith he hath bothe his lady and his love;
His lady, certes, and his wyf also,
The which that lawe of love acordeth to.   90

64 avantate El.

43

And whan he was in this prosperitee,
Hoom with his wyf he gooth to his contree,
Nat fer fro Pedmark, ther his dwellyng was,
Where as he lyveth in blisse and in solas.

Who koude telle, but he hadde wedded be,
The joye, the ese, and the prosperitee,
That is bitwixe an housbonde and his wyf?
A yeer and moore lasted this blisful lyf,
Til that the knyght of which I speke of thus,
That of Kayrrud was cleped Arveragus,   100
Shoope hym to goon and dwelle a yeer or tweyne
In Engelond, that cleped was eek Briteyne,
To seke in armes worshipe and honour,
For al his lust he sette in swich labour;
And dwelled there two yeer, the book seith thus.

Now wol I stynten of this Arveragus,
And speken I wole of Dorigene his wyf,
That loveth hire housbonde as hire hertes lyf,
For his absence wepeth she and siketh,
As doon thise noble wyves whan hem liketh.   110
She moorneth, waketh, wayleth, fasteth, pleyneth.
Desir of his presence hire so destreyneth
That al this wyde world she sette at noght.
Hire freendes, whiche that knewe hir hevy thoght,
Conforten hire in al that ever they may.
They prechen hire, they telle hire nyght and day
That causelees she sleeth hirself, allas!
And every confort possible in this cas
They doon to hire with al hire bisynesse,
Al for to make hire leve hire hevynesse.   120

By proces, as ye knowen everichoon,
Men may so longe graven in a stoon
Til som figure therinne emprented be.

44

So longe han they conforted hire, til she
Receyved hath, by hope and by resoun,
The emprentyng of hire consolacioun,
Thurgh which hir grete sorwe gan aswage.
She may nat alwey duren in swich rage.

  And eek Arveragus, in al this care,
Hath sent hire lettres hoom of his welfare,   130
And that he wol come hastily agayn;
Or elles hadde this sorwe hir herte slayn.

  Hire freendes sawe hir sorwe gan to slake,
And preyde hire on knees, for Goddes sake,
To come and romen hire in compaignye,
Awey to dryve hire derke fantasye.
And finally she graunted that requeste,
For wel she saugh that it was for the beste.

  Now stood hire castel faste by the see,
And often with hire freendes walketh shee,   140
Hire to disporte, upon the bank an heigh,
Where as she many a shipe and barge seigh
Seillynge hir ocurs, where as hem liste go.
But thanne was that a parcel of hire wo,
For to hirself ful ofte, 'Allas!' seith she,
'Is ther no shipe, of so manye as I se,
Wol bryngen hom my lord? Thanne were myn herte
Al warisshed of hise bittre peynes smerte.'

  Another tyme ther wolde she sitte and thynke,
And caste hir eyen dounward fro the brynke.   150
But whan she saugh the grisly rokkes blake,
For verray feere so wolde hir herte quake
That on hire feet she myghte hire noght sustene.
Thanne wolde she sitte adoun upon the grene,
And pitously into the see biholde,
And seyn right thus, with sorweful sikes colde:

'Eterne God, that thurgh thy purveiaunce
Ledest the world by certein governaunce,
In ydel, as men seyn, ye nothyng make.
But, Lord, thise grisly feendly rokkes blake,   160
That semen rather a foul confusioun
Of werk than any fair creacioun
Of swich a parfit wys God and a stable,
Why han ye wroght this werk unresonable?
For by this werk, south, north, ne west, ne eest,
Ther nys yfostred man, ne bryd, ne beest;
It dooth no good, to my wit, but anoyeth.
Se ye nat, Lord, how mankynde it destroyeth?
An hundred thousand bodyes of mankynde
Han rokkes slayn, al be they nat in mynde,   170
Which mankynde is so fair part of thy werk
That thou it madest lyk to thyn owene merk.

Thanne semed it ye hadde a greet chiertee
Toward mankynde; but how thanne may it bee
That ye swiche meenes make it to destroyen,
Whiche meenes do no good, but evere anoyen?
I woot wel clerkes wol seyn as hem leste,
By argumentz, that al is for the beste,
Though I kan the causes nat yknowe.
But thilke God that made wynd to blowe   180
As kepe my lord! This, my conclusioun.
To clerkes lete I al this disputisoun.
But wolde God that alle thise rokkes blake
Were sonken into helle for his sake!
Thise rokkes sleen myn herte for the feere.'
Thus wolde she seyn, with many a pitous teere.

Hire freendes sawe that it was no disport
To romen by the see, but disconfort;

And shopen for to pleyen somwher elles.
They leden hire by ryveres and by welles,   190
And eek in othere places delitables;
They dauncen, and they pleyen at ches and tables.

So on a day, right in the morwe tyde,
Unto a gardyn that was ther bisyde,
In which that they hadde maad hir ordinaunce
Of vitaille and of oother purveiaunce,
They goon, and pleye hem al the longe day.
And this was in the sixte morwe of May,
Which May hadde peynted with his softe shoures
This gardyn ful of leves and of floures.   200
And craft of mannes hand so curiously
Arrayed hadde this gardyn, trewely,
That nevere was ther gardyn of swich prys,
But if it were the verray paradys.
The odour of floures and the fresshe sighte
Wolde han maked any herte lighte
That evere was born, but if to greet siknesse,
Or to greet sorwe, helde it in distresse:
So ful it was of beautee with plesaunce.

At after-dyner gonne they to daunce,   210
And synge also, save Dorigen allone,
Which made alwey hir compleint & hir moone,
For she ne saugh hym on the daunce go
That was hir housbonde and hir love also.
But nathelees she moste a tyme abyde,
And with good hope lete hir sorwe slyde.

Upon this daunce, amonges othere men,
Daunced a squier biforn Dorigen,
That fressher was and jolyer of array,
As to my doom, than is the monthe of May.   220

198 on.

47

He syngeth, daunceth, passynge any man
That is, or was, sith that the world bigan.
Therwith he was, if men sholde hym discryve,
Oon of the beste farynge man on lyve;
Yong, strong, right vertuous, and riche, & wys,
And wel biloved, and holden in greet prys.
And shortly, if the sothe I tellen shal,
Unwityng of this Dorigen at al,
This lusty squier, servant to Venus,
Which that ycleped was Aurelius,   230
Hadde loved hire best of any creature
Two yeer and moore, as was his aventure,
But nevere dorste he tellen hire his grevaunce.
Withouten coppe he drank al his penaunce.
He was despeyred; nothyng dorste he seye,
Save in his songes somwhat wolde he wreye
His wo, as in a general compleynyng;
He seyde he lovede, and was biloved nothyng.
Of swich mater made he manye layes,
Songes, compleintes, roundels, virelayes.   240
How that he dorste nat his sorwe telle,
But langwissheth as a furye dooth in helle;
And dye he moste, he seyde, as dide Ekko
For Narcisus, that dorste nat telle hir wo.
In oother manere than ye heere me seye,
Ne dorste he nat to hire his wo biwreye,
Save that, paraventure, somtyme at daunces,
Ther yong folk kepen hir observaunces,
It may wel be he looked on hir face
In swich a wise as man that asketh grace.   250
But nothyng wiste she of his entente.
Nathelees, it happed, er they thennes wente,
Bycause that he was hire neighebour,

48

And was a man of worshipe and honour,
And hadde yknowen hym of tyme yoore,
They fille in speche; and forth, moore and moore,
Unto this purpos drough Aurelius,
And whan he saugh his tyme, he seyde thus:
   'Madame,' quod he, 'by God that this world made,
So that I wiste it myghte youre herte glade,   260
I wolde that day that youre Arveragus
Wente over the see, that I, Aurelius,
Hadde went ther nevere I sholde have come agayn.
For wel I woot my servyce is in vayn;
My gerdoun is but brestyng of myn herte.
Madame, reweth upon my peynes smerte,
For with a word ye may me sleen or save.
Heere at youre feet God wolde that I were grave!
I ne have as now no leyser moore to seye.
Have mercy, sweete, or ye wol do me deye!'   270
   She gan to looke upon Aurelius.
'Is this youre wyl?' quod she. 'And sey ye thus?
Nev[er]e erst,' quod she, 'ne wiste I what ye mente.
But now, Aurelie, I knowe youre entente,
By thilke God that yaf me soule and lyf,
Ne shal I nevere been untrewe wyf
In word ne werk, as fer as I have wit.
I wol been his to whom that I am knyt.
Taak this for fynal answere as of me.'
But after that in pley thus seyde she: 280
'Aurelie,' quod she, 'by heighe God above,
Yet wolde I graunte yow to been youre love,
Syn I yow se so pitously complayne,
Looke what day that endelong Britayne
Ye remoeve alle the rokkes, stoon by stoon,

273 Neve El.

49

That they ne lette shipe ne boot to goon.
I seye, whan ye han maad the coost so clene
Of rokkes that ther nys no stoon ysene,
Thanne wol I love yow best of any man,
Have heer my trouthe, in al that evere I kan.'   290
'Is ther noon oother grace in yow?' quod he.
'No, by that Lord,' quod she, 'that maked me!
For wel I woot that it shal never bityde.
Lat swiche folies out of youre herte slyde.
What deyntee sholde a man han in his lyf
For to go love another mannes wyf,
That hath hir body whan so that hym liketh?'
Aurelius ful ofte soore siketh.
Wo was Aurelie whan that he this herde,
And with a sorweful herte he thus answerde: 300
'Madame,' quod he, 'this were an inpossible!
Thanne moot I dye of sodeyn deth horrible.'
And with that word he turned hym anon.
Tho coome hir othere freendes many oon,
And in the aleyes romeden up and doun,
And nothyng wiste of this conclusioun,
But sodeynly bigonne revel newe
Til that the brighte sonne loste his hewe;
For th'orisonte hath reft the sonne his lyght—
This is as muche to seye as it was nyght—   310
And hoom they goon in joye and in solas,

291–8 *The majority of manuscripts preserve the order of El. Representatives of four independent lines of descent, however, place 291–2 after 298, an order which seems superior both logically and stylistically, since it not only leads up to a terse climax in 291–2, but also avoids the clash of the repeated Aurelius-Aurelie in 298–9. It is possible that 291–2 were inserted in a margin of the archetype, and that the misplacing appeared at an early stage of the transmission of the text.*

Save oonly wrecche Aurelius, allas!
He to his hous is goon with sorweful herte.
He seeth he may nat fro his deeth asterte;
Hym semed that he felte his herte colde.
Up to the hevene hise handes he gan holde,
And on hise knowes bare he sette hym doun,
And in his ravyng seyde his orisoun.
For verray wo out of his wit he breyde.
He nyste what he spak, but thus he seyde;   320
With pitous herte his pleynt hath he bigonne
Unto the goddes, and first unto the sonne.

   He seyde: 'Appollo, god and governour
Of every plaunte, herbe, tree, and flour,
That yevest, after thy declinacioun,
To ech of hem his tyme and his sesoun,
As thyn herberwe chaungeth lowe or heighe:
Lord Phebus, cast thy merciable eighe
On wrecche Aurelie, which am but lorn.
Lo, lord! my lady hath my deeth y-sworn   330
Withoute gilt, but thy benignytee
Upon my dedly herte have som pitee.
For wel I woot, lord Phebus, if yow lest,
Ye may me helpen, save my lady, best.
Now voucheth sauf that I may yow devyse
How that I may been holpen, and in what wyse.

   Youre blisful suster, Lucina the sheene,
That of the see is chief goddesse and queene
(Though Neptunus have deitee in the see
Yet emperisse aboven hym is she),   340
Ye knowen wel, lord, that right as hir desir
Is to be quyked and lightned of youre fir,

312 wrecched.   329 which that.   337 Luna *written above* Lucina El.
342 lighted.

For which she folweth yow ful bisily,
Right so the see desireth naturelly
To folwen hire, as she that is goddesse
Bothe in the see and ryveres moore and lesse.
Wherfore, lord Phebus, this is my requeste—
Do this miracle, or do myn herte breste—
That now next at this opposicioun
Which in the signe shal be of the Leoun,   350
As preieth hire so greet a flood to brynge
That fyve fadme at the leeste it oversprynge
The hyeste rokke in Armorik Briteyne;
And lat this flood endure yeres tweyne.
Thanne certes to my lady may I seye:
"Holdeth youre heste, the rokkes been aweye."
    Lord Phebus, dooth this miracle for me.
Preye hire she go no faster cours than ye.
I seye, preyeth youre suster that she go
No faster cours than ye thise yeres two.   360
Thanne shal she been evene atte fulle alway,
And spryng flood laste bothe nyght and day.
And but she vouche sauf in swich manere
To graunte me my sovereyn lady deere,
Prey hire to synken every rok adoun
Into hir owene dirke regioun
Under the ground, ther Pluto dwelleth inne,
Or nevere mo shal I my lady wynne.
Thy temple in Delphos wol I barefoot seke.
Lord Phebus, se the teeris on my cheke,   370
And of my peyne have som compassioun.'
And with that word in swowne he fil adoun,
And longe tyme he lay forth in a traunce.
    His brother, which that knew of his penaunce,

Up caughte hym, and to bedde he hath hym broght.
Dispeyred in this torment and this thoght
Lete I this woful creäture lye—
Chese he, for me, wheither he wol lyve or dye.
   Arveragus, with heele and greet honour,
As he that was of chivalrie the flour,   380
Is comen hoom, and othere worthy men.
O blisful artow now, thou Dorigen,
That hast thy lusty housbonde in thyne armes,
The fresshe knyght, the worthy man of armes,
That loveth thee as his owene hertes lyf!
Nothyng list hym to been ymaginatyf,
If any wight hadde spoke, whil he was oute,
To hire of love; he hadde of it no doute.
He noght entendeth to no swich mateere,
But daunceth, justeth, maketh hire good cheere.   390
And thus in joye and blisse I lete hem dwelle,
And of the sike Aurelius I wol yow telle.
   In langour and in torment furyus
Two yeer and moore lay wrecche Aurelyus,
Er any foot he myghte on erthe gon;
Ne confort in this tyme hadde he noon,
Save of his brother, which that was a clerk,
He knew of al this wo and al this werk;
For to noon oother creäture, certeyn,
Of this matere he dorste no word seyn.   400
Under his brest he baar it moore secree
Than evere dide Pamphilus for Galathee.
His brest was hool withoute for to sene,
But in his herte ay was the arwe kene.
[And] wel ye knowe that of a sursanure
In surgerye is perilous the cure,

378 wher. *This reading satisfies the metre.*   392 wol I telle.   405 As El.

53

But men myghte touche the arwe, or come therby.
His brother weep and wayled pryvely,
Til atte laste hym fil in remembra[u]nce
That whiles he was at Orliens in Fraunce,   410
As yonge clerkes, that been lykerous
To reden art[es] that been curious,
Seken in every halke and every herne
Particuler sciences for to lerne—
He hym remembred that, upon a day,
At Orliens in studie a book he say
Of magyk natureel, which his felawe,
That was that tyme a Bacheler of Lawe,
Al were he ther to lerne another craft,
Hadde prively upon his desk ylaft;   420
Which book spak muchel of the operaciouns
Touchynge the eighte and twenty mansiouns
That longen to the moone, and swich folye
As in oure dayes is nat worth a flye—
For Hooly Chirches feith in oure bileve
Ne suffreth noon illusioun us to greve.
And whan this book was in his remembraunce,
Anon for joye his herte gan to daunce,
And to hymself he seyde pryvely:
'My brother shal be warisshed hastily;   430
For I am siker that ther be sciences
By wh[i]c[h]e men make diverse apparences,
Swiche as thise subtile tregetours pleye.
For ofte at feestes have I wel herd seye
That tregetours, withinne an halle large,
Have maad come in a water and a barge,
And in the halle rowen up and doun.
Somtyme hath semed come a grym leoun;

412 artz El. *The metre here requires a dissyllable.*   432 whce El.

54

And somtyme floures sprynge as in a mede;
Somtyme a vyne and grapes white and rede;   440
Somtyme a castel, al of lym and stoon;
And whan hym lyked, voyded it anon.
Thus semed it to every mannes sighte.

    Now thanne conclude I thus, that if I myghte
At Orliens som oold felawe yfynde
That hadde this moones mansions in mynde,
Or oother magyk natureel above,
He sholde wel make my brother han his love.
For with an apparence a clerk may make,
To mannes sighte, that alle the rokkes blake   450
Of Britaigne weren yvoyded everichon,
And shippes by the brynke comen and gon,
And in swich forme enduren a wowke or two.
Thanne were my brother warisshed of his wo;
Thanne moste she nedes holden hire biheste,
Or elles he shal shame hire atte leeste.'

    What sholde I make a lenger tale of this?
Unto his brotheres bed he comen is,
And swich confort he yaf hym for to gon
To Orliens that he up stirte anon,   460
And on his wey forthward thanne is he fare
In hope for to been lissed of his care.

    Whan they were come almoost to that citee,
But if it were a two furlong or thre,
A yong clerk romynge by hymself they mette,
Which that in Latyn thriftily hem grette,
And after that he seyde a wonder thyng.
'I knowe,' quod he, 'the cause of youre comyng.'
And er they ferther any foote wente,
He tolde hem al that was in hire entente.   470

    442 hem.   453 day. Cf. wyke, 587.

This Briton clerk hym asked of felawes
The whiche that he had knowe in olde dawes,
And he answerde hym that they dede were,
For which he weep ful ofte many a teere.

Doun of his hors Aurelius lighte anon,
And with this mágicien forth is he gon
Hoom to his hous, and maden hem wel at ese.
Hem lakked no vitaille that myghte hem plese.
So wel arrayed hous as ther was oon
Aurelius in his lyf saugh nevere noon.   480

He shewed hym, er he wente to sopeer,
Forestes, parkes ful of wilde deer;
Ther saugh he hertes with hir hornes hye,
The gretteste that evere were seyn with eye.
He saugh of hem an hondred slayn with houndes,
And somme with arwes blede of bittre woundes.

He saugh, whan voyded were thise wilde deer,
Thise fauconers upon a fair ryver
That with hir haukes han the heroun slayn.

Tho saugh he knyghtes justyng in a playn.   490
And after this he dide hym swich plesaunce
That he hym shewed his lady on a daunce,
On which hymself he daunced, as hym thoughte.

And whan this maister that this magyk wroughte
Saugh it was tyme, he clapte hise handes two,
And farewel! al oure revel was ago.
And yet remoeved they nevere out of the hous
Whil they saugh al this sighte merveillous,
But in his studie, ther-as hise bookes be,
They seten stille, and no wight but they thre.   500

To hym this maister called his squier,
And seyde hym thus: 'Is redy oure soper?
Almoost an houre it is, I undertake,

56

Sith I yow bad oure soper for to make,
Whan that thise worthy men wenten with me
Into my studie, ther-as my bookes be.'
  'Sire,' quod this squier, 'whan it liketh yow,
It is al redy, though ye wol right now.'
'Go we thanne soupe,' quod he, 'as for the beste.
This amorous folk somtyme moote han hir reste.'   510
  At after-soper fille they in tretee
What somme sholde this maistres gerdoun be
To remoeven alle the rokkes of Britayne
And eek from Gerounde to the mouth of Sayne.
  He made it straunge, and swoor, so God hym save,
Lasse than a thousand pound he wolde nat have.
Ne gladly for that somme he wolde nat goon.
  Aurelius, with blisful herte anoon,
Answerde thus: 'Fy on a thousand pound!
This wyde world, which that men seye is round,   520
I wolde it yeve, if I were lord of it.
This bargayn is ful dryve, for we been knyt.
Ye shal be payed trewely, by my trouthe!
But looketh now, for no necligence or slouthe
Ye tarie us heere no lenger than tomorwe.'
  'Nay,' quod this clerk, 'have heer my feith to borwe.'
  To bedde is goon Aurelius whan hym leste,
And wel ny al that nyght he hadde his reste.
What for his labour and his hope of blisse,
His woful herte of penaunce hadde a lisse.   530
  Upon the morwe whan that it was day,
To Britaigne tooke they the righte way,
Aurelius and this mágicien bisyde,
And been descended ther they wolde abyde.
And this was, as thise bookes me remembre,
The colde, frosty sesoun of Decembre.

57

Phebus wax old, and hewed lyk latoun,
That in his hoote declynacioun
Shoon as the burned gold with stremes brighte;
But now in Capricorn adoun he lighte,   540
Where as he shoon ful pale, I dar wel seyn.
The bittre frostes with the sleet and reyn
Destroyed hath the grene in every yerd.
Janus sit by the fyr with double berd,
And drynketh of his bugle-horn the wyn;
Biforn hym stant brawen of the tusked swyn,
And 'Nowel!' crieth every lusty man.

  Aurelius in al that evere he kan
Dooth to his maister chiere and reverence,
And preyeth hym to doon his diligence   550
To bryngen hym out of his peynes smerte,
Or with a swerd that he wolde slitte his herte.

  This subtil clerk swich routhe had of this man
That nyght and day he spedde hym that he kan
To wayten a tyme of his conclusioun;
This is to seye, to maken illusioun
By swich a[n] apparence of jogelrye—
I ne kan no termes of astrologye—
That she and every wight sholde wene & seye
That of Britaigne the rokkes were aweye,   560
Or ellis they were sonken under grounde.
So atte laste he hath his tyme yfounde
To maken hise japes and his wrecchednesse
Of swich a supersticious cursednesse.
Hise tables Tolletanes forth he brought,
Ful wel corrected, ne ther lakked nought
Neither his collect ne hise expans yeeris,
Ne hise rootes, ne hise othere geeris,

As been his centris, and hise argumentz,
And hise proporcioneles convenientz   570
For hise equacions in every thyng.
And by his 8 speere in his wirkyng
He knew ful wel how fer Alnath was shove
Fro the heed of thilke fixe Aries above,
That in the 9 speere considered is;
Ful subtilly he hadde kalkuled al this.

Whan he hadde founde his firste mansioun,
He knew the remenaunt by proporcioun,
And knew the arisyng of his moone weel,
And in whos face, and terme, and everydeel;   580
And knew ful weel the moones mansioun
Acordaunt to his operacioun;
And knew also hise othere observaunces
For swiche illusiouns and swiche meschaunces
As hethen folk useden in thilke dayes.
For which no lenger maked he delayes,
But thurgh his magik, for a wyke or tweye,
It semed that alle the rokkes were aweye.

Aurelius, which that yet despeired is
Wher he shal han his love or fare amys,   590
Awaiteth nyght and day on this myracle;
And whan he knew that ther was noon obstacle,
That voyded were thise rokkes everychon,
Doun to hise maistres feet he fil anon,
And seyde: 'I, woful wrecche Aurelius,
Thanke yow, lord, and lady myn Venus,
That me han holpen fro my cares colde.'
And to the temple his wey forth hath he holde,
Where as he knew he sholde his lady see.
And whan he saugh his tyme, anon right hee,   600

576 he kalkuled. *The reading of* El *does not satisfy the metre.*

With dredful herte and with ful humble cheere
Salewed hath his sovereyn lady deere.

   'My righte lady,' quod this woful man,
'Whom I moost drede and love as I best kan,
And lothest were of al this world displese,
Nere it that I for yow have swich disese
That I moste dyen heere at youre foot anon,
Noght wolde I telle how me is wo bigon.
But certes outher moste I dye or pleyne.
Ye sle me giltlees for verray peyne.   610
But of my deeth thogh that ye have no routhe,
Avyseth yow er that ye breke youre trouthe.
Repenteth yow, for thilke God above,
Er ye me sleen bycause that I yow love.
For, madame, wel ye woot what ye han hight—
Nat that I chalange anythyng of right
Of yow, my sovereyn lady, but youre grace—
But in a gardyn yond, at swich a place,
Ye woot right wel what ye bihighten me
And in myn hand youre trouthe plighten ye   620
To love me best. God woot, ye seyde so,
Al be that I unworthy am therto.
Madame, I speke it for the honour of yow
Moore than to save myn hertes lyf right now,
I have do so as ye comanded me;
And if ye vouche sauf, ye may go see.
Dooth as yow list; have youre biheste in mynde,
For, quyk or deed, right there ye shal me fynde.
In yow lith al to do me lyve or deye—
But wel I woot the rokkes been aweye.'   630

   He taketh his leve, and she astoned stood;
In al hir face nas a drope of blood.

613 *Possibly* Ra[3] *has the original reading here,* Bethenketh yow.

She wende nevere han come in swich a trappe.
'Allas,' quod she, 'that evere this sholde happe!
For wende I nevere by possibilitee
That swich a monstre or merveille myghte bee.
It is agayns the proces of nature.'
   And hoom she goth a sorweful creature;
For verray feere unnethe may she go.
She wepeth, wailleth, al a day or two,   640
And swowneth, that it routhe was to see.
But why it was, to no wight tolde shee,
For out of towne was goon Arveragus.
But to hirself she spak and seyde thus,
With face pale and with ful sorweful cheere,
In hire compleynt, as ye shal after heere.
   'Allas,' quod she, 'on thee, Fortune, I pleyne,
That unwar wrapped hast me in thy cheyne;
For which t'escape woot I no s[o]cour
Save oonly deeth or dishonour.   650
Oon of thise two bihoveth me to chese.
But nathelees, yet have I levere to lese
My lif than of my body have a shame,
Or knowe myselven fals, or lese my name.
And with my deth I may be quyt, ywis.
Hath ther nat many a noble wyf er this,
And many a mayde, yslayn hirself, allas!
Rather than with hir body doon trespas?
Yis, certes, lo, thise stories beren witnesse,
Whan xxx tirauntz ful of cursednesse   660
Hadde slayn Phidoun in Atthenes at feste,
They comanded hise doghtres for t'areste
And bryngen hem biforn hem in despit,
Al naked, to fulfille hir foul delit,

633 have.   649 scour El.   653 to have.   661 atte.   662 doghtren.

And in hir fadres blood they made hem daunce
Upon the pavement. God yeve hem myschaunce!
For which thise woful maydens, ful of drede,
Rather than they wolde lese hir maydenhede,
They prively been stirt into a welle,
And dreynte hemselven, as the bookes telle.   670

    They of Mecene leete enquere and seke
Of Lacedomye fifty maydens eke,
On whiche they wolden doon hir lecherye.
But was ther noon of al that compaignye
That she nas slayn, and with a good entente
Chees rather for to dye than assente
To been oppressed of hir maydenhede.
Why sholde I, thanne, to dye been in drede?

    Lo, eek, the tiraunt Aristoclides,
That loved a mayden, heet Stymphalides,   680
Whan that hir fader slayn was on a nyght,
Unto Dianes temple goth she right,
And hente the ymage in hir handes two,
Fro which ymage wolde she nevere go.
No wight ne myghte hir handes of it arace
Til she was slayn, right in the selve place.

    Now sith that maydens hadden swich despit
To been defouled with mannes foul delit,
Wel oghte a wyf rather hirselven slee
Than be defouled, as it thynketh me.   690

    What shal I seyn of Hasdrubales wyf,
That at Cartage birafte hirself hir lyf?
For whan she saugh that Romayns wan the toun,
She took hir children alle, and skipte adoun
Into the fyr, and chees rather to dye
Than any Romayn dide hire vileynye.

    Hath nat Lucresse yslayn hirself, allas!

At Rome, whan she oppressed was
Of Tarquyn, for hire thoughte it was a shame
To lyven whan she had lost hir name?   700
    The sevene maydens of Melesie also
Han slayn hemself for drede and wo
Rather than folk of Gawle hem sholde oppresse.
Mo than a thousand stories, as I gesse,
Koude I now telle as touchynge this mateere.
    Whan Habradate was slayn, his wyf so deere
Hirselven slow, and leet hir blood to glyde
In Habradates woundes depe and wyde,
And seyde: "My body, at the leeste way,
Ther shal no wight defoulen, if I may."   710
    What sholde I mo ensamples heerof sayn,
Sith that so manye han hemselven slayn
Wel rather than they wolde defouled be?
I wol conclude that it is bet for me
To sleen myself than been defouled thus.
I wol be trewe unto Arveragus,
Or rather sleen myself in som manere,
As dide Demociones doghter deere
Bycause that she wolde nat defouled be.
    O Cedasus, it is ful greet pitee   720
To reden how thy doghtren deyde, allas!
That slowe hemself for swich manere cas.
    As greet a pitee was it, or wel moore,
The Theban mayden that for Nichanore
Hirselven slow, right for swich manere wo.
    Another Theban mayden dide right so;
For oon of Macidonye hadde hire oppressed,
She with hire deeth hir maydenhede redressed.
    What shal I seye of Nicerates wyf,

        702 verray drede. *This reading satisfies the metre.*

63

That for swich cas birafte hirself hir lyf?   730
  How trewe eek was to Alcebiades
His love, rather for to dyen chees
Than for to suffre his body unburyed be!
  Lo, which a wyf was Alceste!' quod she.
'What seith Omer of goode Penalopee?
Al Grece knoweth of hire chastitee.
  Pardee, of [Laodomya] is writen thus,
That whan at Troie was slayn Protheselaus,
No lenger wolde she lyve after his day.
  The same of noble Porcia telle I may;   740
Withoute Brutus koude she nat lyve,
To whom she hadde al hool hir herte yeve.
  The parfit wyfhod of Arthemesie
Honured is thurgh al the Barbarie.
  O Teuta queene, thy wyfly chastitee
To alle wyves may a mirour bee.
  The same thyng I seye of Bilyea,
Of Rodogone, and eek Valeria.'
  Thus pleyne[d] Dorigene a day or tweye,
Purposynge evere that she wolde deye.   750
But nathelees, upon the thridde nyght,
Hoom cam Arveragus, this worthy knyght,
And asked hire why that she weepe so soore.
And she gan wepen ever lenger the moore.
  'Allas,' quod she, 'that evere I was born!
Thus have I seyd,' quod she, 'thus have I sworn.'
And toold hym al, as ye han herd bifore;
It nedeth nat reherce it yow namoore.
  This housbonde, with glad chiere, in freendly wyse,
Answerde and seyde as I shal yow devyse: 760
'Is ther oght elles, Dorigen, but this?'

732 love that.   737 Lacedomya El.   749 pleyne El.   755 was I.

'Nay, nay,' quod she, 'God helpe me so as wys!
This is to muche, and it were Goddes wille.'
   'Ye, wyf,' quod he, 'lat slepen that is stille.
It may be wel, paraventure, yet today.
Ye shul youre trouthe holden, by my fay!
For God so wisly have mercy upon me,
I hadde wel levere ystiked for to be
For verray love which that I to yow have,
But if ye sholde youre trouthe kepe & save.   770
   Trouthe is the hyeste thyng that man may kepe.'
   But with that word he brast anon to wepe,
And seyde: 'I yow forbede, up peyne [of] deeth,
That nevere, whil thee lasteth lyf ne breeth,
To no wight telle thou of this aventure—
As I may best, I wol my wo endure—
Ne make no contenance of hevynesse,
That folk of yow may demen harm or gesse.'
   And forth he cleped a squier and a mayde:
'Gooth forth anon with Dorigen,' he sayde,   780
And bryngeth hire to swich a place anon.'
They take hir leve and on hir wey they gon,
But they ne wiste why she thider wente;
He nolde no wight tellen his entente.

   Paraventure an heepe of yow, ywis,
Wol holden hym a lewed man in this,
That he wol putte his wyf in jupartie.
Herkneth the tale er ye upon hire crie.
She may have bettre fortune than yow semeth;
And whan that ye han herd the tale, demeth.   790

   This squier, which that highte Aurelius,
On Dorigen that was so amorus,
Of aventure happed hire to meete

773 of El *alone omits.*

Amydde the toun, right in the quykkest strete,
As she was bown to goon the wey forth right
Toward the gardyn ther as she had hight.
And he was to the gardyn-ward also;
For wel he spyed whan she wolde go
Out of hir hous to any maner place.
But thus they mette, of aventure or grace,   800
And he saleweth hire with glad entente,
And asked of hire whiderward she wente.

  And she answerde, half as she were mad:
'Unto the gardyn, as myn housbonde bad,
My trouthe for to holde, allas! allas!'

  Aurelius gan wondren on this cas,
And in his herte hadde greet compassioun
Of hire and of hire lamentacioun,
And of Arveragus, the worthy knyght,
That bad hire holden al that she had hight,   810
So looth hym was his wyf sholde breke hir trouthe.
And in his herte he caughte of this greet routhe,
Considerynge the beste on every syde,
That fro his lust yet were hym levere abyde
Than doon so heigh a cherlyssh wrecchednesse
Agayns franchise and alle gentillesse.
For which in fewe wordes seyde he thus:

  'Madame, seyeth to youre lord Arveragus,
That sith I se his grete gentillesse
To yow, and eek I se wel youre distresse,   820
That him were levere han shame (and that were routhe)
Than ye to me sholde breke thus youre trouthe,
I have wel levere evere to suffre wo
Than I departe the love bitwix yow two.
I yow relesse, madame, into youre hond
Quyt every serement and every bond

66

That ye han maad to me as heer biforn,
Sith thilke tyme which that ye were born.
My trouthe I plighte, I shal yow never repreve
Of no biheste. And heere I take my leve,   830
As of the treweste and the beste wyf
That evere yet I knew in al my lyf.'

But every wyf be war of hire biheeste!
On Dorigene remembreth, atte leeste.
Thus kan a squier doon a gentil dede
As wel as kan a knyght, withouten drede.

She thonketh hym upon hir knees al bare,
And hoom unto hir housbonde is she fare,
And tolde hym al, as ye han herd me sayd.
And be ye siker he was so weel apayd   840
That it were inpossible me to wryte.

What sholde I lenger of this cas endyte?
Arveragus and Dorigene his wyf
In sovereyn blisse leden forth hir lyf.
Nevere eft ne was ther angre hem bitwene.
He cherisseth hire as though she were a queene,
And she was to hym trewe for everemoore.
Of thise folk ye gete of me namoore.

Aurelius, that his cost hath al forlorn,
Curseth the tyme that evere he was born.   850
'Allas,' quod he, 'allas, that I bihighte
Of pured gold a thousand pound of wighte
Unto this philosophre! How shal I do?
I se namoore but that I am fordo.
Myn heritage moot I nedes selle,
And been a beggere. Heere may I nat dwelle,
And shamen al my kynrede in this place,
But I of hym may gete bettre grace.

848 thise two.
67

But nathelees, I wole of hym assaye,
At certeyn dayes, yeer by yeer, to paye,   860
And thanke hym of his grete curteisye.
My trouthe wol I kepe, I wol nat lye.'

    With herte soor he gooth unto his cofre,
And broghte gold unto this philosophre,
The value of fyve hundred pound, I gesse,
And hym bisecheth, of his gentillesse,
To graunte hym dayes of the remenaunt;
And seyde: 'Maister, I dar wel make avaunt,
I failled nevere of my trouthe as yit.
For sikerly my dette shal be quyt   870
Towardes yow, howevere that I fare,
To goon a-begged in my kirtel bare.
But wolde ye vouche sauf, upon seuretee,
Two yeer or thre for to respiten me,
Thanne were I wel; for elles moot I selle
Myn heritage. Ther is namoore to telle.'

    This philosophre sobrely answerde,
And seyde thus, whan he thise wordes herde:
'Have I nat holden covenant unto thee?'
    'Yes, certes, wel and trewely,' quod he.   880
'Hastow nat had thy lady as thee liketh?'
'No, no,' quod he, and sorwefully he siketh.
'What was the cause? Tel me if thou kan.'
    Aurelius his tale anon bigan,
And tolde hym al, as he han herd bifoore.
It nedeth nat to yow reherce it moore.

    He seide: 'Arveragus, of gentillesse,
Hadde levere dye in sorwe and in distresse
Than that his wyf were of hir trouthe fals.'
The sorwe of Dorigen he tolde hym als;   890

885 ye.
68

How looth hire was to been a wikked wyf,
And that she levere had lost that day hir lyf,
And that hir trouthe she swoor thurgh innocence:
She nevere erst hadde herd speke of apparence.
'That made me han of hire so greet pitee.
And right as frely as he sente hire me,
As frely sente I hire to hym ageyn.
This al and som; ther is namoore to seyn.'

This philosophre answerde: 'Leeve brother,
Everich of yow dide gentilly til oother.   900
Thou art a squier, and he is a knyght.
But God forbede, for his blisful myght,
But if a clerk koude doon a gentil dede
As wel as any of yow, it is no drede!

Sire, I releesse thee thy thousand pound
As thou right now were cropen out of the ground
Ne nevere er now ne haddest knowen me.
For, sire, I wol nat taken a peny of thee
For al my craft, ne noght for my travaille.
Thou hast ypayed wel for my vitaille.   910
It is ynogh, and farewel, have good day!'
And took his hors, and forth he goth his way.

Lordynges, this questioun thanne wolde I aske now,
Which was the mooste fre, as thynketh yow?
Now telleth me, er that ye ferther wende.
I kan namoore; my tale is at an ende.

913 wol.

NOTES

331. *Frankeleyn.* A franklin was a free man but not of noble birth. His social status varied according to circumstance. Franklins were often wealthy, landowners, and ranked as gentlemen. This particular Franklin on the pilgrimage corresponds to the well-to-do country squire of later days. He held responsible offices in the state, and was now travelling in the company of the important Man of Law. See Introd., 'The Franklin and his Tale'.

332. *heed.* It is the practice in this edition to retain the reading of the Ellesmere MS (El) wherever it gives sense. *heed* is a unique reading, but here in fact it offers a more telling image than the reading *berd* of the other manuscripts. It suggests the roundness of the daisy and the crimson underside of the white petals through the picture of a white head of hair crowning a ruddy countenance.

333. *complexioun . . . sangwyn.* These are terms of medieval physiology. Man's temperament depended on which of the four humours was predominant in him—sanguine, phlegmatic, choleric, or melancholy, characterized respectively by the predominance of blood, phlegm, choler, black bile. These four humours were themselves combinations of two of the four elements—hot, cold, dry, wet—from which all creatures were held to be composed. Sanguine was hot and wet, phlegm cold and wet, choleric hot and dry, melancholy cold and dry. These combinations, determining the nature of a man, changed according to the influence of the planets (see Appendix IV). As the dominant humour affected the appearance, 'complexioun', originally a technical term (Latin *complexion–em,* 'combination'), came to have its modern meaning.

336–8. *Epicurus . . . felicitee parfit.* This is an over-simplified statement of the ethics of the Greek philosopher, Epicurus

71

Notes

(341–270 B.C.). The gist of his teaching occurs in a letter to Menoeceus in which he states: 'We declare pleasure to be the beginning and end of the blessed life . . . a right conception of pleasure itself conduces to right living, since it is not possible to live pleasantly without living wisely and well and righteously.'

355. *lord and sire.* i.e. he presided at the sessions of the Justices of the Peace.

356. *knyght of the shire.* i.e. he represented his county in Parliament.

LINK F

683–5. 'I had rather that he were a man . . . than have land worth twenty pounds a year.' The Franklin's monetary comparison betrays his bourgeois origin.

THE FRANKLIN'S TALE

1–7. The Franklin introduces his tale as an old Breton lay, describing the circumstances of composition and the method of performance of such works in times gone by. He claims a source which has not yet been discovered; in fact, it has been repudiated. See Introd., pp. 28–30.

The extant 'Breton lays' belong to a specific literary genre, first popularized by Marie de France in the late twelfth century by the tales she recalled and wrote down from the songs of Breton minstrels, which, she stated, she had formerly heard to the accompaniment of an instrument, harp or viol. The actual origin of Marie's poems is not known. She described the songs as being written to keep fresh the memory of some noteworthy incident or story. Music was probably inseparable from such compositions, and equally as important as the words. The relation between these original lyrics and the narrative lays extant can only be conjectured. A likely suggestion is that the Breton minstrel, in the manner of programme notes today, first recounted the story, which occasioned the Breton song, in prose and in the language of the country in which he found himself, for the Breton minstrels wandered far; and Marie retold the plots of the stories in her French poems, which were intended for recital and reading.

Marie's lays are short narrative poems of a romantic

character, written under Celtic influence. Her stories are usually based on a single incident, neither conventional nor courtly, often passionate, full of irony, closely associated with magic. Two of her lays, *Lay le Freyne* and *Sir Launfal*, were translated into English before the middle of the fourteenth century, and appear, together with *Sir Orfeo*, a Middle English poem of the same type, in a manuscript which Chaucer possibly saw—the Auchinleck MS, compiled in London about 1330. By the second half of the fourteenth century literary fashions had changed in England, and the Breton lay type was comparatively unknown. It is typical of Chaucer's imaginative attention to detail that he gave this outmoded kind of narrative to the white-haired country gentleman, the Franklin. Possibly in consequence of *The Franklin's Tale* there was a revival of interest. At least four more Middle English imitations of the Breton lays appeared—*Sir Degaré, Émaré, The Earl of Toulous* and *Sir Gowther*.

Though the Franklin's introductory lines bear vague resemblances to scattered passages in Marie de France's lays, their identity in content and certain correspondences in vocabulary and rhyme establish their close connection with a prologue associated with *Sir Orfeo* and the Middle English version of the *Lay le Freyne*, of which they seem to be a suave and polished summary (cf. *Sir Orfeo*, ed. A. J. Bliss, Oxford, 1954, pp. xlvi–xlvii, and 2–3).

8–18. In this apologetic introduction the Franklin begs to be excused for his plain style since he is unversed in the art of rhetoric, i.e. the art of elegant and persuasive composition.

Rhetoric was the second of the seven liberal arts, and with grammar and logic comprised the trivium, the basis of the curriculum in medieval schools and universities. Rhetoric had a long history. Its principles, first formulated for the training of orators among the ancient Greeks, had been applied also to poetry by the Romans, and transmitted by them in treatises such as the anonymous *Rhetorica ad Herennium* (*c.* 85 B.C. This was wrongly attributed to Cicero in the Middle Ages), Cicero's *De Inventione*, Quintilian's *Institutio Oratoria* (*c.* A.D. 95), works destined to have an incalculable influence on the composition of verse and prose for more than sixteen hundred years. Countless medieval textbooks (e.g. Matthieu de Vendôme's *Ars Versificatoria* and Geoffrey de Vinsauf's *Poetria Nova*, which Chaucer satirized in *The Nun's Priest's Tale*, though he used it seriously enough elsewhere) did little more than repeat the directions from classical antiquity.

Manuals on rhetoric prescribed the selection and arrangement of material, methods of amplification in the development of a theme and of abbreviation, and ways to embellish with ornaments of style. In their illustrations they provided a storehouse of examples ready for most requirements. Few medieval writers are free from the influence of rhetoric. Chaucer usually proceeds in accordance with the commonly accepted traditions of composition. An elaborate introduction was recommended. The Franklin begins with a long digression on a successful marriage full of apothegms (short 'wise' sayings) and far from the main narrative, which is chiefly concerned with the virtues of integrity and generosity. He amplifies his story in the customary manner—by descriptions, by comparisons, by personifications, by apostrophe and exclamation, by periphrasis, and by presenting one and the same idea in different ways for emphasis.

'Colours', from Latin *colores*, is a technical term for rhetorical embellishments. Sixty-four such stylistic ornaments were described in the *Rhetorica ad Herennium*, Book IV, and later adopted in medieval treatises on rhetoric. Geoffrey de Vinsauf classified these devices as 'difficult' and 'easy'. The difficult ornaments (or *tropes*) involve a departure from the ordinary significance of words, and include such figures as metaphor (*translatio*), hyperbole (*superlatio*), expressions with a hidden meaning, allegorical or ironical (*permutatio*), circumlocution (*circuito*), onomatopoeic coining (*nominatio*), a descriptive term used for a proper name (*pronominatio*), the substitution of an attributive word for the name of a thing (*metonymy*), the mention of a part for the whole or vice versa (*synecdoche*). The easy devices, which deal both with the arrangement of words and with processes of thought, are generally described as 'colours', but in his disavowal of the use of colours the Franklin obviously intends to include all contrivance for literary effect.

The Franklin's statement is not borne out by the lines he

speaks. In fact, the great majority of the recognized tropes and colours can be illustrated from his tale. These are well worth examination since attention to them will give awareness of the verbal fabric and movement of the poem. The Franklin's very disavowal is couched in rhetorical terms and is full of artifice. Such a modest introductory confession of shortcomings (*diminutio*) was itself the kind of beginning strongly recommended by the rhetoricians as a means of gaining sympathy from the start. Lines 10–19 amplify the theme by varying the presentation of it (*interpretatio*). Lines 13–14 consist of circumlocution by oblique references to poetry in the allusion to the home of the Muses and to rhetoric in the name of its greatest authority (*metonymy*). The repudiation is completed by a play on words (*adnominatio*).

Geoffrey de Vinsauf recommended that the full use of tropes and colours should be limited to the 'high' or elevated style. They are most profuse in the many monologues and dialogues of *The Franklin's Tale*. Of all the characters Dorigen speaks with the greatest passion and intensity. In her apostrophe to 'Eterne God' (157–85), which consists largely of an accumulation of reasoning (*frequentatio*), advanced through a series of rhetorical questions (*interrogatio*) and amplified by *interpretatio*, she emphasizes her argument by pausing over it (*commoratio* 166–8, 175–6), by making it forceful through antithesis (*contentio*) of words (161–2) and ideas (171–5) and through the emphatic repetition (*traductio*) of the keyword 'rokkes', and she concludes strikingly (180–4) with a play on the word 'conclusioun' (*adnominatio*), a brief summing up (*conclusio*) and a double exclamation. Her later apostrophe to Fortune (647–748) is no less mannered. After presenting her dilemma (*divisio*), she cites twenty-two *exempla* as points in her argument (*frequentatio*), amplifying each by *interpretatio*, with five instances of *interrogatio*, three of *exclamatio*, two of self-questioning (*ratiocinatio*), and with one suggested answer (*sub°ectio*). Aurelius's confession of love (259–70) is an extended innuendo (*significatio*), evidently conveying to Dorigen more than it actually says. The other speeches might be similarly analysed.

It is true that the intervening narrative is for the most part simple and direct, yet even here the Franklin introduces tropes

75

Notes

[e.g. *translatio* throughout, *circuito* 308–10, *permutatio* 234, *pro-nominatio* 229, *superlatio* 203–4, 221–2], figures of diction [paradox through *contentio* 86, *sententia* 66–7, 122–3, *correctio* (substitution of a more suitable expression than the one just used) 87, *interrogatio* 95–7, *gradatio* (repetition of the closing word of one clause as the opening word of the next) 86–7, *transitio* (a brief statement of what has been said and what is to follow) 106–7, 391–2, *articulus* (a succession of words without conjunctions) 111, 225, 239–40, *exclamatio* 382, *definitio* (a brief explanation) 556–7, *occupatio* (brief reference to a subject under cover of passing it over) 840–2, 885–6, etc.], and figures of thought [*interpretatio* 29, *conformatio* or *prosopopoeia* (personification) 57–8, *significatio* 110, *notatio* (delineation of character) 224–6, *sermocinatio* (imaginary discourse) 430ff., *licentia* (censorious speech) 423–4, 563–4, *brevitas* (concise expression) 457–462, *distributio* (detailing) 481–93, 565–71, 577–82]. See also Notes, 200ff., 537–47.

The purpose of the Franklin's declaration is easily discoverable in the wider context of the drama of the Canterbury pilgrimage. It is a profession of loyalties in the guise of appeasement. The Franklin was imitating the Squire whom he admired and who had immediately preceded him with a similar avowal:

> Myn Englissh eek is insufficient,
> It moste been a rethor excellent,
> That koude his colours longynge for that art . . . (F 37–9)

Both Squire and Franklin were probably reacting to the Host's brusque attack on the Clerk:

> Youre termes, youre colours, and youre figures,
> Keepe hem in stoor til so be that ye endite
> Heigh style . . .   (E 16–18)

13. A marginal note in El refers to Persius and gives the relevant quotation from the *Satires*: '*nec in bicipite pernaso me memini sompniasse*'.

18. This is a nine-syllabled line. Possibly the four-syllabled *rethoryke* was the original reading.

Notes

21. *Armorik.* As we are told in Geoffrey of Monmouth's *Historia Regum Britanniae* and in many old chronicles, Armorica (from *Ar vor*, 'land by the sea') was the ancient name for Brittany. Maximian renamed the new country Little Britain, or 'Britain beyond the sea' in memory of the greater Britain (cf. 102). Chaucer thus begins with a deliberate and scholarly archaism appropriate for the tale which 'thise olde gentil Britouns in hir dayes' first told.

22–6. The knight is first presented as a typical lover behaving in accordance with the conventions of courtly love. These conventions, which made almost a religion of love and demanded a highly-stylized set of human relationships, arose from a mistakenly literal interpretation of Ovid's ironical *Ars Amatoria* as it had been developed in the Troubadour poetry of the twelfth and thirteenth centuries, systematized in such textbooks as the *De Arte Honesti Amandi* of Andreas Capellanus, and given full and methodical literary treatment in the French love allegory of the *Roman de la Rose*, which was begun probably about 1237 by Guillaume de Lorris and finished towards the end of the thirteenth century by Jean de Meun. Chaucer himself translated a large part of the *Roman*, and was greatly influenced in the majority of his works by its psychology. In accordance with this tradition, the lover adored from afar a beautiful lady of noble kindred, often the wife of another, but he dared not tell his love. Inspired by her, he undertook great deeds for her sake. All his worth was derived from her. His principal rôle was one of suffering and despair, of timidity, and of the utmost submission to the lady's will. Such a relationship had already been fully described in *The Knight's Tale* and alluded to by the Squire (F 523ff.), and the Franklin continues the theme, with the same stock vocabulary of *service, peyne, penaunce, pitee, meke obeysaunce,* etc.

26. *oon the faireste.* Possibly in imitation of the Latin idiom *unus* + superlative.

30–1. Cf. *Squire's Tale,* F 562–3:

> And I so loved hym for his obeisaunce,
> And for the trouthe I demed in his herte.

Notes

32–4. Cf. *Knight's Tale*, A 3080–3:

> That ye shul of youre grace upon hym rewe,
> And taken hym for housbonde and for lord.
> Lene me youre hond, for this is oure accord.
> Lat se now of youre wommanly pitee.

44. '. . . in order not to bring shame upon his status (as a husband).'

46. *gentillesse*: 'magnanimity'. *Gentil*, and its compounds, *gentilly*, *gentillesse*, words often used in *The Canterbury Tales*, are charged with associations and capable of almost unlimited extension. Their significance varies with the character and circumstances of the user. The repetition of *gentil-* towards the end of *The Franklin's Tale* quietly registers the personal triumph of the Franklin over the Host, who had rudely interrupted his commendation of the Squire. 'Straw for youre gentillesse!' the Host says, when the Franklin, adopting the Squire's favourite epithet, praises the Squire for acquitting himself 'gentilly' and wishes that his own son were more like the Squire than the gambler he is, preferring to

> '. . . talken with a page
> Than to comune with any gentil wight
> Where he myghte lerne gentillesse aright'.

The wise Franklin forbears to reply directly to the Host, but immediately begins a tale adopted from 'thise olde gentil Britouns' of which the climax is to be a comparison of different manifestations of 'gentillesse'.

The Franklin extends the meaning of the word beyond the usage of the Squire. To the Squire 'gentil' denotes good breeding, refinement of manners, sensibility (F 195, 265, 451–2, 479, 546, 622), and with this interpretation the Franklin applies the epithet to the Squire himself. The Host has some of the proletarian sensitiveness to class distinctions, and is probably rather irritated by what he considers to be the Franklin's social pretensions (see Introd.). *Gentil*, moreover, is with the Host a favourite term which he uses to all and sundry—to the Manciple, Summoner, Pardoner, Roger the Cook, the Shipman. Even today it is customary at a certain level of society and in certain

78

walks of life to refer to all men and women as ladies and gentlemen. The Host has already been disappointed and irritated by the sermonizing of the Wife of Bath. The Wife had groped towards a definition of 'gentillesse'—her church-going and her scholar-husband's reading had left some impression upon her:

> . . . he is gentil that dooth gentil dedis.   (D 1170)

> Looke who that is moost vertuous alway,
> Pryvee and apert, and moost entendeth ay
> To do the gentil dedes that he kan;
> Taak hym for the grettest gentil man.   (D 1113–16)

> God . . . wole that of hym we clayme oure gentillesse.
> (D 1129–30)

These are but reiterations of the medieval commonplace of the identity of true nobility and virtue, which had been expressed by Seneca, Juvenal, Boethius, Jean de Meun, Dante, and countless others. The Franklin, whose tale was greatly in-fluenced and in part prompted by the words of the Wife of Bath, illustrates her contention that *gentillesse* depends on a man's self, and not on his social position or ancestry. He ex-pounds the term further, as the quality of one with a ready sympathy and awareness of the sufferings of others, a generosity without self-interest, an unwavering fidelity to one's word. All these one would expect from the noble traditions of the aristo-cracy, but they are by no means confined to men of high birth. A clerk and a squire can behave as 'gentilly' as a knight. To Chaucer *gentillesse*, at its highest human level, was a profound spiritual quality, a blend of the virtues of the aristocratic tradition and of medieval Christianity. He writes of it so in the poem *Gentilesse* (Robinson, p. 536).

53ff. Having described the conditions for a successful marriage, 36–52, the Franklin adds extended variations on the theme in a long digression from his story. The repeated word *maistrie*, in context with terms of *lordshipe* and *soveraynetee*, shows the reason why. The Franklin must have disagreed strongly with the Wife of Bath's insistence that a wife should dominate over her husband, and the words of her outpouring were still ringing in his ears: e.g.

Notes

> And whan that I hadde geten unto me,
> By maistrie, al the soveraynetee . . .
> After that day we hadden never debaat. (D 817–22)

> Wommen desiren have sovereynetee
> As wel over hir housbond as hir love,
> And for to been in maistrie hym above. (D 1038–9)

The Clerk's counterpoise had been his tale of the patient Griselda's excessive submission to her husband concluded by an ironical wish for the Wife of Bath, E 1171–2:

> Whos lyf and al hire secte God mayntene
> In heigh maistrie.

It remained for the Franklin to set the marriage relationship in just perspective. He resumes the Clerk's themes of patience and forbearing, but he stresses that these must be on both sides.

There is little doubt that this part of the Franklin's narrative is the direct outcome of the Wife of Bath's, for the vocabulary is used with the same nuances. When the same words occur elsewhere in Chaucer's poetry, as the concordance will show, their associations are different. See J. P. S. Tatlock and A. G. Kennedy, *A Concordance to the Complete Works of Geoffrey Chaucer and the Romaunt of the Rose*, Washington, 1927.

57–8. Though not expressed with such imaginative personification in the known parallels, e.g. *Roman de la Rose* (ed. E. Langlois, Paris, 1914–24) 9439–42, 8451–3, the idea is a literary commonplace. Cf. *Knight's Tale*, A 1625–6:

> Ful sooth is seyd that love ne lordshipe
> Wol noght, his thankes, have no felaweshipe.

65–7. It is impossible to identify 'thise clerkes' for the theme of the power of patience was a commonplace which not only had scriptural authority (cf. Proverbs xvi. 32, James i. 4) but also occurred in one of the basic school textbooks of the Middle Ages, *The Distichs of Cato*. Though Chaucer introduced it elsewhere (e.g. *Tale of Melibee*, Robinson, p. 180, *Troilus and Criseyde*, iv. 1584), in this particular context it is charged with the memory of *The Clerk's Tale*.

73. *constellacioun*. The configuration of the planets, in

80

constant change through the motions of the spheres and their own rotations, were believed to affect every part of a man's life, his body, disposition, health, and fortune. See Appendix IV.

74. *chaungynge of complexioun*: 'change in disposition'. See note to *GP* 333.

81–2. A clever touch of dramatic irony.

85ff. The Franklin plays with the paradox that the Knight after marriage was both the servant and lord of his wife, and she in turn his wife and mistress. This twist of thought had many literary antecedents. Cf. *Roman de la Rose*, 9449–54.

90. The courtly love convention, which held love to be possible only outside marriage, militated against happiness in wedded life and fidelity in wife and husband. See note to 22–6. The Franklin was a pillar of society. In his compromise he not only corrected the assertions of the Wife of Bath, but also reconciled the courtly tradition with the teaching of the Church. The continuance of love and a happy marriage founded on mutual respect and toleration were made possible by the Knight's yielding of his masculine prerogative of lordship and his wife's resolve, expressed as Griselda might have expressed it, to be his 'humble trewe wyf'. It would seem likely that the Franklin was here voicing Chaucer's own opinion, for the same solution is offered elsewhere. Cf. *Knight's Tale*, A 3103–4:

> And Emelye hym loveth so tendrely
> And he hire serveth al so gentilly.

It is implied at the end even of *The Wife of Bath's Tale*, for after the husband's submission—

> I put me in youre wise governance   (D 1231)

we are told of the wife:

> And she obeyed hym in every thyng
> That myghte doon hym plesance or likyng. (D 1255–6)

93. *Pedmark*. This is a definite locality in Brittany, named and clearly described. J. S. P. Tatlock, *The Scene of the Franklin's Tale Visited*, shows that the 'Pedmark' found in the best manuscripts refers to Penmarc'h, a commune in the s.w. corner of the

Dept. of Finistère, not far from Quimper, and a little to the south of Brest. At the headland of Penmarc'h the shore at low tide consists of great expanses of low reef, with occasional rock masses, and not a mile to sea stretches a fearful chain of granite rocks—rocks which are highly characteristic of this section of the coast of Brittany, and which were to occasion the plot of *The Franklin's Tale* (see 151, 160, 183, etc.).

It is quite possible that Chaucer might have reached Brittany on one of his campaigns or missions abroad, or have had a first-hand description of this coast from one of his friends who had campaigned there, or from one of the merchants he met in the port of London. Chaucer's Shipman knew 'every cryke in Britayne', and all the tides, currents, and dangers of the coast from Bordeaux to England (see *GP*, A 396–7, 401–9). Professor E. G. R. Taylor has shown, however, in *The Haven Finding Art*, pp. 131–7, that some early pilot book might well have been the inspiration for the choice of setting, for there was much traffic along this coast, particularly of ships bringing to England the wines of Bordeaux and Spain. The earliest surviving pilot book (known as a 'rutter', Fr. *routier*, a book showing the route or course), which might have been derived from a fourteenth-century manuscript, makes specific mention of the coast between the Rock of Gibraltar and Penmarc'h Point, noting the tides, depths, currents, and rocks, and giving information about the relationship between the moon and the full sea in that area. See note to 348–54. The earliest tide table known, found in the great Catalan Atlas of c. 1375, which Chaucer could possibly have seen at the French court, gives data about Penmarc'h, and its last entry is for the Mouth of the Seine (cf. *FT*, 514).

Chaucer's 'grisly rokkes blake' might well have taken shape in his imagination from some chart. A coloured map of Brittany belonging to the time of Henry IV, fully marked between the port of Brest and the Raz de Sein, exists in the British Museum, MS Sloane 557, f.26. Sixteenth-century Breton tide tables still extant indicate high water by a rock symbol.

95–7. This rhetorical question gains in significance when it is considered in the context of *The Canterbury Tales*. The deliberate

Notes

verbal echoes in the Franklin's sincere admiration seem to be intended as antidote to the Merchant's venomous irony. The Merchant, disgusted with his own marriage, had told a savage tale of an old knight deceived by his young wife, whom he had wedded because he wanted to know:

> of thilke blisful lyf
> That is bitwixe an housbonde and his wyf.　(E 1259-60)

> The blisse which that is bitwixe hem tweye
> Ther may no tonge telle, or herte thynke.　(E 1340-1)

98-103. This is reminiscent of lines in the previous story told by the Squire:

> This lasteth lenger than a yeer or two.　(F 574)

> And resoun wolde eek that he moste go
> For his honour . . .　(F 591-2)

But the Franklin's narrative was to be one with a difference.

The profession of knighthood entailed deeds of chivalry and active adventure as well as loyalty to a lady. Medieval romances reiterate the fear that love might cause a knight to linger in sloth at home. Arveragus is here behaving as a true knight should.

100. *Kayrrud.* This name of Celtic origin is possibly an English attempt at a phonetic spelling of the earlier form of the Breton name which has developed into modern 'Kerru', signifying a red mansion or town. The first element, Celtic *Kaer*, *Caer*, still to be found in Welsh and Cornish names, denotes a place of varying size from a fortress to a town. Professor Tatlock (*The Scene of the Franklin's Tale Visited*) suggests that the second element, 'red', may be explained by the brick of Roman buildings. The town may have received its name from the many Gallo-Roman remains which still survive in the district. The place-name, Kerru, is found elsewhere in Brittany. Though it does not occur in this particular region of Penmarc'h today, it may well have been known there in the fourteenth century.

100. *Arveragus.* A Latinized form of a Celtic name, which helps to give remoteness to a story professedly told of long ago.

83

Notes

There is a character with this name in Shakespeare's *Cymbeline*, the action of which is laid in Roman Britain.

102. *eek Briteyne*. Cf. 21 and note.

105. *the book seith thus*. This reference is to an unknown source.

107. *Dorigene*. Elsewhere 'Dorigen', a Celtic name, probably pronounced with a hard g. Droguen, or Dorigien, was the name of the wife of Alain I of Brittany.

110. A sly Chaucerian touch. The Franklin had just listened to the Squire's long and pitiful account of the falcon, which had elaborated upon a lady's grief at separation (F 412ff.).

111. Cf. *Knight's Tale*, A 2822–6:

> For in swich cas wommen have swich sorwe,
> Whan that hir housbondes ben from hem ago,
> That for the moore part they sorwen so,
> Or ellis fallen in swich maladye,
> That at the laste certeinly they dye.

122–3. The Franklin's figure is different from the usual proverbial one which is to be found in his likely source, *Il Filocolo*: 'by constant dripping soft water wears away hard stone'.

157–85. This long impassioned invocation has a profundity of thought not repeated elsewhere in *The Franklin's Tale*, and this is reflected in the poetry. In the elaboration of the problem of evil, the accumulating emphasis from the repeated allusions to the 'grisly feendly rokkes blake' (160, 170, 183) and the fall at the climax to 'sonken into helle' (184) make the black rocks seem a veritable emanation from evil. The thought, and the heightened style and diction of the introductory lines at once recall Palamon's invocation in *The Knight's Tale*,

> O crueel goddes that governe
> This world with byndyng of youre word eterne . . .
>
> (A 1303–4)

Dorigen no less than Palamon is calling the Almighty to task, though she does it more gently. The ultimate source for both the questioning thought and the style is perhaps Boethius's *De Consolatione Philosophiae*, which Chaucer himself translated (Robinson, pp. 319–84). Cf.

84

Notes

I m.v. O thou governour, governynge alle thynges by certein ende, whi refusestow oonly to governe the werkes of men by duwe manere? Why suffrestow . . . ? . . . We men, that ben noght a foul partie, but a fair partie of so greet a werk . . .

III m. ix. O thow Fadir . . . that governest this world by perdurable resoun . . .

157. *purveiaunce.* Boethius, *De Consolatione,* IV, pr. vi, explains God's Providence. The Godhead is One and Simple, transcendent, outside all created things, as well as holding them in being. All things, all changing natures, all forms, causes, movements, what has been or can be, the whole finite universe of heterogeneity and multifariousness, lie within the mind of the Godhead. This plan of all things in the Divine thought is called Providence, or 'Purveiaunce'.

170. *nat in mynde.* The possible bathos after the sustained eloquence of the preceding lines suggests that Dorigen's fluency was running away with her.

172. *merk.* Cf. Genesis i. 27: *ad imaginem suam,* A.V. 'in his own image'. In Middle English versions of Matthew xxii. 20, *merk* was used to translate Latin *imago* = the impression on a coin, which explains how it came to mean 'likeness'.

178–81. *argumentz, causes, conclusioun.* These are scholastic terms of logic. Dorigen plays on the word *conclusioun* in 181.

182. Cf. *Knight's Tale,* A 1323–4

> The answere of this lete I to dyvynys,
> But wel I woot that in this world greet pyne ys.

192. *tables.* Until the seventeenth century this was the name of Backgammon. The game was played by two opponents on a table marked with twenty-four partitions. Throwing two or three dice, each player tried to bring his fifteen men first through the partitions and across the table.

198. *the sixte morwe of May.* There is comparable particularizing in *The Knight's Tale,* A 1462–3: in May,/The thridde nyght. In medieval calendars two days each month, and sometimes three, were evil days, called 'Egyptian', because of the plagues God sent to Egypt, or 'dismal' from Latin *dies mali.* May 6 does

not appear among these with the regularity of May 3. It is listed
however in a manuscript of the time of Henry VI, described by
R. Chambers, *The Book of Days*, among the days perilous 'for to
take any sickness in, or to be hurt in, or to be wedded in, or to
take any journey upon, or to begin any work on, that he would
well speed'. May 6 is not mentioned in the great medieval en-
cyclopaedia of scientific information, the *De Proprietatibus Rerum*
of Bartholomaeus, but further information has been added in
Batman uppon Bartholome his Booke De Proprietatibus Rerum (1582).
'Divers perilous dayes' are given, May 7, 15, 20, and 'These
not so evill, the thirde the Sixt'. If this tradition went back to the
fourteenth century, by selecting May 3 and 6, Chaucer might
have meant to imply that the fortune these particular days
brought was not entirely evil.

200ff. Like the gardens in *The Knight's Tale*, A 1051ff., *The
Squire's Tale*, F 392ff., *The Merchant's Tale*, E 2029ff., and count-
less other gardens in medieval writings, this particular one has
a literary ancestry in the vision of the beautiful garden in the
Roman de la Rose where the god of love and all his company are
making merry. This garden in turn owed its details to the
descriptions of the ideal landscape (*locus amoenus*) provided in
treatises on rhetoric, not intended to represent reality but to add
a rich décor. The rhetorical descriptions of a beautiful natural
site in spring, shaded, full of flowers and scents, with bird-song
and often a caressing breeze, easily developed into the medieval
pictures of the Earthly Paradise. That Chaucer was ultimately
indebted to the rhetoricians is perhaps indicated by his use of
peynted (199), a striking metaphor today but a medieval
commonplace. When illustrating the figure of metaphor
Geoffrey de Vinsauf quoted its Latin equivalent *pingere* in the
phrase 'Tempora veris pingere flore solum', 'The spring
seasons paint the earth with flowers.'

From among the innumerable gardens thus descended, four
seem to have given immediate inspiration for the one described
by the Franklin—the gardens in the probable source, *Il Filocolo*,
the garden in the *Teseida* (the source of *The Knight's Tale*) and,
most direct of all, the garden in G. de Machaut's *Le Dit Dou
Vergier*. In Machaut's poem there are not only close parallels to
200–9, but also his garden is visited by a lover sorrowing at the

Notes

absence of his beloved, and hoping in vain to dismiss his sorrow by watching the revelry of others.

206. Cf. *Squire's Tale*, F 395–6:
> But nathelees it was so fair a sighte
> That it made alle hire hertes for to lighte.

218. Aurelius is introduced first as a type before he takes on individuality. As a living model in appearance, accomplishments, and condition, the Franklin had before him the young Squire of the Canterbury pilgrimage whom he greatly admired —'a lovyere and a lusty bacheler' (A 80):

> Embrouded was he, as it were a meede
> Al ful of fresshe floures, whyte and reede. (A 89–90)

> He was as fressh as is the month of May. (A 92)

> He koude songes make and wel endite,
> Juste and eek daunce, and weel purtreye and write.
> So hoote he lovede that by nyghtertale
> He sleep namoore than dooth a nyghtyngale. (A 95–8)

The Franklin has also just listened to the Merchant's belittling account of a licentious squire called Damien, which might explain the stress laid on Aurelius's virtue (224–6), intended to correct the bad impression. By his portrait he would recall the two noble young lovers of *The Knight's Tale*, one of whom, Arcite, became a squire.

Chaucer, the poet, had also his own life and reading to draw upon. He too had once been a squire, accomplished in singing and dancing and with a love of gay attire. But it is always hard in Chaucer's poetry to establish the boundary between convention and personal experience. There are many similarities between the Squire and both the ideal lover and Mirth in Guillaume de Lorris's part of the *Roman de la Rose*. Moreover, the actual portrait of Aurelius has many points of resemblance to that of Arcite, as it is found not only in *The Knight's Tale* but also in the *Teseida*, its source. See Introd., p. 21.

220. *than is the monthe of May*. This particular simile is a commonplace, found in the Troubadour and Trouvère poetry, and often repeated by Chaucer. It may be significant that in medieval calendars May was often represented as a young

Notes

squire on horseback, in brightly coloured and embroidered attire, very like the Squire of the *General Prologue*.

224. *Oon of the beste farynge man.* This is a mixed construction, vacillating between 'Oon the beste farynge' and 'Oon of . . . men'. Cf. 26 and note.

228. This situation is closely paralleled in *The Knight's Tale* by Emily's ignorance of the two young knights languishing for love of her, a detail adopted from the *Teseida*.

229. *servant to Venus.* Aurelius was a worthy lover. Cf. 224–6 with Arcite's dying words, *Knight's Tale*, A 2787–91:

> To speken of a servaunt proprely,
> With alle circumstances trewely—
> That is to seyn, trouthe, honour, knyghthede,
> Wysdom, humblesse, estaat, and heigh kynrede,
> Fredom, and al that longeth to that art.

232. Cf. *Knight's Tale*, A 1446: And thre yeer in this wise his lif he ladde.

234. This difficult line probably means that he suffered without measure, i.e. not in measured doses, but from the fountain head. The obscure 'cup' metaphor has been variously interpreted: 'under difficulties', 'in full draught'. W. H. French ingeniously suggests that since 'to drink the woes of love' was a common figure, and since 'penaunce' is the usual term for the torment of falling in love without due encouragement, 'penaunce' might be understood as 'sorrow due to love'. Since this suffering was purely inward, no cup was needed—hence the line might be interpreted: 'In secrecy he suffered bitter pain from love.' (See *Modern Language Notes*, lx, p. 477.)

238. The same complaint is made by a lover in the *Teseida* (iv. 68).

239–40. The Squire herein resembles the young Chaucer, who in fact popularized the French roundel form in English poetry. Cf. *Legend of Good Women* (Robinson, p. 492):

> And many an ympne for your halydayes,
> That highten balades, roundels, virelayes.   (F 422–3)
>
> He hath maad many a lay . . .   (F 430)

Notes

These songs, courtly lyrical poems on love with a fixed form, were the literary fashion of the second half of the fourteenth century. The meaning of 'layes' here is different from that in 2, where the reference was to a kind of narrative poem. The later fourteenth century did not clearly know what a lay was, and used the term loosely for a song, sometimes the song of a bird, but more often as a synonym for complaint. Cf. *Merchant's Tale*, E 1881, where Damien wrote of his sorrow 'in manere of a compleynt or a lay'. Among the short poems of Chaucer are many complaints—*A Complaint to his Lady, The Complaint of Mars, The Complaint of Venus, A Balade of Complaint. Anelida and Arcite* consists largely of an elaborate complaint.

Virelayes were of the roundel type of composition—originally sung to a dance in a 'ronde', or circle, with two units, a verse and a refrain. There is no known Chaucerian virelay extant, but a roundel is introduced at the end of *The Parliament of Fowls* (Robinson, p. 318), with two of the three opening lines repeated in the middle of the song, and all three repeated at the end. In adopting these fixed lyrical forms Chaucer was imitating such French poets as Guillaume de Machaut, Froissart, and Eustache Deschamps.

242. Hell was the regular abiding-place of the three Furies, cf. *Troilus and Criseyde*, i. 9: Thow cruwel Furie, sorwynge evere yn peyne; iv. 22-3: O ye Herynes [i.e. Furies] . . . That endeles compleignen evere in pyne. Chaucer's conception of the Furies undergoing torment is different from that of such classical writers as Virgil, Ovid, and Statius, who depict them as wild savage creatures who do the tormenting. Chaucer may have known Dante's treatment, e.g. *Inferno*, ix. 46ff. (trans. D. L. Sayers, Penguin edition):

There on the right Alecto howls, and lo!
Megaera on the left; betwixt them wails
Tisiphone . . .
They beat their breasts, and tore them with their nails,
Shrieking so loud . . .

243-4. The Ellesmere MS gives the marginal reference '*Methamorphosios*'. Ovid tells in *Metamorphoses* iii. 370ff. how Echo, finding the arrogant Narcissus inaccessible to her, hid herself in the woods and wasted away for grief, until nothing was left of her but her voice.

255. *And hadde*. Where there was no ambiguity, the pronoun subject was often omitted in Middle English.

257. *this*. The reading of the majority of the MSS. *his* makes the better sense, but Hg agrees with El.

280-90. This passage shows an imaginative penetration of the mind of Dorigen, and a rich complication of thought. She had a very common human weakness, that of not being able to give a flat refusal where it would cause pain. She compromised herself by adding the unnecessary words, in an attempt to soften the effects of the blow and to part friends. Her immediate thought of the rocks proves even more surely than her rejection of Aurelius's suit that she was entirely devoted to Arveragus, for her longing for their removal was only to ensure her husband's safe return. She was still under the influence of her earlier obsession (cf. 149–85). Superficially her speech begins like that of many a haughty lady of romance imposing conditions on her lover, and Aurelius perversely accepts it as such. Underneath, Dorigen was trying to emphasize the enduring love she felt for her husband, which nothing could change, just as nothing could remove the rocks which menaced her husband's life. (The rocks have taken on another symbolical meaning.) Her practical down-to-earth conclusion in 293–7, in complete contradiction of the convention of courtly love, proves how little she intended Aurelius to understand her literally and to attempt the task.

304-5. Here is a very natural touch, giving a most effective contrast. After this dramatic scene, Dorigen's friends come up to her and, knowing nothing of the tension of the situation upon which they have very nearly intruded, they proceed straight-way to dance. Cf. the same skilful introduction of contrast at 311–13.

308-10. The plain and simple explanation following the poetic conceit (*circuito*) is typically Chaucerian in its humorous anticlimax. Cf. *Troilus and Criseyde*, ii. 904–5:

> The dayes honour, and the hevenes yë,
> The nyghtes foo—al this clepe I the sonne—.

Notes

Circuito was a common figure of speech in lines defining the time. Cf. *Merchant's Tale*, E 1795-7:

> Parfourned hath the sonne his ark diurne;
> No lenger may the body of hym sojurne
> On th'orisonte.

The same sort of description is found in Dante's work, e.g. *Purgatory*, vii. 59-60 (trans. D. L. Sayers, Penguin edition):

> While the horizon's ring
> Seals down the day, until the morning come.

323-71. Aurelius's invocation is a typical late Middle English commixture of pagan ideas and medieval science such as is found at length in *The Knight's Tale*. 'Phebus' (328), originally an epithet signifying 'bright, life-giving', is another name for Apollo. Aurelius invokes simultaneously the ancient god and the planet, the sun. Such a blend of mythical and astrological ideas had a long tradition, going back at least to the second century A.D. A popular compendium of such information for literary use in the late fourteenth and fifteenth centuries was Boccaccio's *De Genealogia Deorum*. The moving position of the sun in the heavens determines the change in the seasons and all plant life. A more elaborate form of this introduction occurs in *Teseida*, iii. 5-7, which might well have inspired this passage.

325. *declinacioun.* See Appendix IV.

327. *herberwe:* 'lodging'. This is a reference to the sun's residence in the different astrological mansions.

337. *suster, Lucina.* The Ellesmere MS gives the gloss *Luna*. Aurelius is referring to the triform goddess of the threefold universe—heaven above, earth below, and the regions of darkness and gloom beneath—best known as Luna (Moon) in the heavens, Diana on earth, and Proserpina (Hecate) in the underworld. As Diana she was the goddess of chastity, as Lucina she helped women in childbirth. Aurelius needed Luna, but he could hardly have prayed to the one who was also Lucina-Diana to help him to win the wife of another. Like many men seeking favour, he thought to win it through the brother's persuasion.

91

Notes

341ff. Aurelius knew that the waters depended on the moon, and that the moon depended on solar light.

348-54. The poet's own knowledge is rather hidden behind the apparent naïveté of Aurelius's solution. The sun's power is greatest in its own mansion of Leo (see Appendix IV) and Aurelius was willing to wait three months to have the sun in this sign for the miracle. In May, the time of his prayer, the sun is in Taurus and the moon in opposition in Scorpio. Two other signs, Gemini and Cancer, precede Leo. When the sun is in Leo, the moon is in opposition in Aquarius, a most appropriate sign for the desired watery miracle. The sun affects the tides like the moon, though its influence is less than half as great as the moon's. The tides are highest when the sun and moon are in conjunction (i.e. new moon) or in opposition (i.e. 180° apart at full moon), for then the two influences reinforce each other and produce the fortnightly spring tides. With the spring tides the rise is higher and the ebb lower than at other times. Aurelius wanted a tide which at ebb would still leave the rocks covered. At high tide the level of the water must be at least thirty feet ('fyve fadme') above the top of the rocks. The current *Nautical Almanac* gives 24 feet as the mean range of the spring tides at Brest, which is not far from Penmarc'h. It seems probable that Chaucer based his 'fyve fadme' on soundings for the coast of Brittany given in some pilot book or chart. Cf. 93 and note.

Misled by his mistaken idea of the universe, Aurelius argued that the miracle of having the same spring tide for two years could be achieved by the moon's keeping a uniform pace with the sun, and like the sun, revolving round the earth once a year, and not once in every twenty-eight days.

365-7. Aurelius's prayer is parallel to Dorigen's, 183-4. In *The Knight's Tale*, Emily prayed to Diana in similar terms, cf. A 2298-9:

> To whom bothe hevene and erthe and see is sene,
> Queene of the regne of Pluto derk and lowe.

Cf. also A 2081-2:

> Hir [Diana's] eyen caste she ful lowe adoun,
> Ther Pluto hath his derke regioun.

92

Notes

According to Greek mythology, Pluto (Hades), king of the underworld, abducted Proserpina to be his queen. On her mother's entreaty she was allowed to spend two-thirds of the year in the world, at the end of which she returned to rule the subterranean realm as the dark goddess of death.

369. *Delphos*. Chaucer's name for Delphi is perhaps from the accusative form, or by confusion with Delos. Apollo was born on the island of Delos, but the chief of all his oracles was at Delphi, on a spur of Mount Parnassus. The idea of vowing a pilgrimage was medieval.

377-8. There is a similar detached withdrawing from extravagant conduct in *The Merchant's Tale*, E 1781:

But there I lete hym wepe ynogh and pleyne.

379-94. There is a striking contrast between the active happy life of Arveragus and the languishing sickness of Aurelius. Cf. the love-sickness and despair of Arcite in *The Knight's Tale*, A 1361-82. The medieval descriptions of the torments of unrequited love have a uniformity in countless romances and lyrics. The symptoms are lack of sleep, loss of appetite, paleness, pining, swooning, weeping and wailing. Cf. 22-9, and note to 22-6.

380. Cf. Theseus in *The Knight's Tale*, A 982:

And in his hoost of chivalrie the flour.

401. Secrecy was an essential condition of courtly love.

402-4. A marginal note in El gives the reference: *Pamphilus ad Galatheam*, and quotes *vulneror et clausum porto sub pectore telum* ('I am wounded with a dart which I bear hidden in my breast'). Pamphilus was the hero of a medieval Latin poem, *Pamphilus de Amore*.

409-10. The local colour is remarkably true to fact. The university of Orleans had a world-wide reputation for the study of law, which after 1300 survived as its only Faculty. Chaucer's friend, Deschamps, was once a student there, and described the typical life of a Bachelor of Law in his *Miroir de Mariage* (*Œuvres*, ix. 2105ff.). According to H. Rashdall, *Universities of Europe in the Middle Ages* (1936, ii, p. 149), there were ninety-five bachelors of civil and canon law in residence at

Notes

Orleans in 1394, reading for a mastership or a doctorate, and meanwhile lecturing, or giving some instruction. Orleans was also a gathering-place for astrologers in the fourteenth century.

416–17. From what follows it seems that this particular book was one of astrology. Natural magic was held by many, including St Thomas Aquinas, to be a legitimate science, as opposed to black magic, which invoked diabolic aid and worked by means of evil spirits. Through natural magic, based on a close knowledge of the changing positions of the planets and stars, and of the varying influences of their different combinations, the astrologer could utilize the marvellous influence of the heavenly bodies. Images or verbal charms composed under the appropriate constellations could receive and store up their mysterious energy and power. Natural science was most useful in medicinal prescriptions, in meteorological prognostications, and in the election of suitable times for any enterprise. Cf. Appendix IV.

422–3. For the magical significance of the mansions of the moon, see Appendix IV.

423–6. Cf. 564 and note.

431ff. The brother with characteristic medieval credulity makes no distinction between control of the elements through astrological lore and illusions produced as if by magic for entertainment at court. Lines 431–4 recall the comments on the magic horse in *The Squire's Tale*, F 217–19:

> . . . it is rather lyk
> An apparence ymaad by som magyk,
> As jogelours pleyen at thise feestes grete.

A 'tregetour' by sleight of hand and contrivance of machinery produced effects which seemed the result of enchantment. Cf. *The House of Fame*, 1277–81 (Robinson, p. 294):

> Ther saugh I Colle tregetour
> Upon a table of sycamour
> Pleye an uncouth thyng to telle;
> Y saugh him carien a wynd-melle
> Under a walsh-note shale.

Illusions were the common stock of many medieval tales.

Notes

Virgil was revered as one of the greatest of magicians working such wonders. Stories were told of how the great theologian, Albertus Magnus, produced the illusion of spring in midwinter to delight his guests. *Il Filocolo*, the suggested source of *The Franklin's Tale*, contains a similar 'miracle'—a flowering garden in January. Among the wonders seen at the Great Khan's court and described in *The Travels of Sir John Mandeville* are parallels to all the visions which Aurelius enjoyed in the Clerk's study (482–93)—imaginary hunts, jousting, dancers who disappeared as mysteriously as they had come. It is very possible that Chaucer himself, or one of his friends, had witnessed such scenic marvels as the brother recalls (435–42). Mrs Loomis (see Bibliography) has produced evidence to show that in the royal palace in Paris in 1378 and 1389 similar effects were seen by hundreds of people in interludes performed during sumptuous feasts. A late fourteenth-century manuscript of the *Chronique de Charles V* not only describes the dramatic entertainment of 1378 which enacted scenes from the First Crusade but also gives an illustration which shows the stage properties—a barge and a castle!— which it describes as appearing as if by magic, wonderfully contrived so as to be moved about quietly on wheels. Froissart in his *Chronicles* tells of comparable entertainment in 1389 in which a ship and the fortifications of Troy suddenly appeared.

465ff. It is amusing to note the stages by which the Clerk wins Aurelius's confidence, and how he gradually leads up to the point of bargaining. He first meets the brothers casually on the road, yet soon shows that he knows the purpose of their journey. After inviting them into a magnificently appointed house, which surprises even the rich client, he provides examples of his skill, shrewdly selected to appeal to a young squire, whose own pastimes are hunting, hawking, jousting and dancing. These culminate in the dance in which the lover feels that he is dancing with his lady. Just when the vision has whetted Aurelius's appetite intolerably, it is summarily dismissed. The Clerk then entertains his guests to a splendid supper, but when they are replete and prepared to relax he suddenly changes his tone, and shocks Aurelius into such a desire for reconciliation with this magician who can attain his lady for him that he casts all prudence to the winds, and promises to pay a sum which he realizes later would ruin him.

488. *ryver*. A hawking ground on the bank of a river.

495-6. It seems likely that the Franklin means it to be understood that the Clerk works his illusions through spirits. Cf. *The Tempest*, iv. i: 'Our revels now are ended.' Chaucer's own credulity is questionable. The clap of the hands could have dismissed the spirits, or equally well have given the signal to his assistant to finish.

502-4. Cf. 478. One is reminded of Chaucer's portrait of the Franklin himself—of his well-stocked home (*GP*, A 345-6), and of the sharpness of his tone with offending servants (*GP*, A 351-2).

510. The quick change of tone is very effective, from sharpness to his inferiors to playful badinage with his guests.

514. The mouths of the two rivers, Gironde and Seine, are almost equidistant from the Point of Penmarc'h. Again the local colour is strikingly accurate. Cf. 92-3 and note.

528. Very true to life.

537-47. This dating by purely decorative statement is a fine example of medieval literary art, in which rhetorical tropes and colours intermingle in rich profusion. Lines 537-43 elaborate 323-7, describing the season in terms of the position of the sun along the ecliptic, contrasting its 'hoote declynacioun' at the summer solstice in the sign of Cancer with its position at the winter solstice in Capricorn. Despite the classical name of Phebus, the reference here is wholly astrological. The style is typically Chaucerian, cf. *Troilus and Criseyde*, v. 8-9: 'The gold-ytressed Phebus . . . with his bemes clene.'

Lines 544-7 reinforce the description of the season with an indoor scene. Janus, the Latin god of all going-out and coming-in, commonly represented with two faces placed back to back and looking in opposite directions (sometimes both bearded, sometimes one clean-shaven), was the god of entrance into a new division of time, and looked back to the old year and forward to the new. From him the first month of the year

Notes

derived its name, January. Janus had power not only on land, but also on sea, and from him sprang all wells, rivers, and streams, associations which might partly explain his appearance here. Chaucer's unobtrusive learning was far-reaching.

R. Tuve, in *Seasons and Months*, has clearly demonstrated the likeness of this whole passage to familiar season motifs in medieval manuscript illuminations of Calendars and Books of Hours, and in sculpture. In many calendar series the declining sun takes its course through Capricorn over a landscape of bare trees and brown earth. Janus often appears in January, sitting at a table on which stand vessels for a feast, with two servants, one reaching for the empty goblet, symbol of the old year, one handing a full goblet, symbol of the new year, as at the north door, west façade of Amiens Cathedral; at a table drinking from a horn and holding a loaf on a Norman lead font at Brookland, Kent; eating and drinking with a boar's head before him in a fourteenth-century MS of the Peterborough Psalter (Corpus Christi College, Cambridge); standing at a table on which is a boar's head, with musicians to left and to right, one fiddling, one harping, in a fourteenth-century MS at the British Museum (Royal 19 C 1).

Chaucer might here have been describing one particular manuscript illumination but, if so, the exact source of this word picture is not known. One suspects that his description might, in fact, be a composite from memory. Usually the figure warming himself by the fire belongs to February. There is also the difficulty of date, whether Janus here represents December, cf. 536, or January. Janus usually belongs to January, but in fourteenth-century England there was a national cycle, represented by the Gorleston Psalter, in which Janus feasts in December. According to an older tradition the year started on Christmas Day. In *The Franklin's Tale* Janus (cf. 'janitor') probably represents the turn of the year.

Professor Tatlock has calculated that the date of the miracle was January 2 or 3, a date corresponding to that in *Il Filocolo*. The sun reached Capricorn (540) on December 12 in 1361 and for about 125 years thereafter. The Clerk watched night and day (554), and only 'atte laste' (562) found a time propitious for his magic.

Notes

547. *Nowel.* A shout of joy, or public acclamation, from Latin *natalis* 'birthday', and usually associated with Christmas, but not necessarily only with December 25. The great medieval festivities lasted from Christmas Day to Twelfth Night (January 6). The same cry is uttered on January 1 in the fourteenth-century romance, *Sir Gawain and the Green Knight*.

554-5. '. . . he made all possible haste to be on the alert for an opportunity for his practical experiment.'

kan is present where one would expect a past tense. It is possible that in this context *kan* is a variant of *gan*, preterite, 'began'. The sense would then be that 'he so pressed on that he began to look out for an opportunity . . .'

555. Cf. *Squire's Tale*, F 129-30:

> He wayted many a constellacion
> Er he had doon this operacion.

564. *a supersticious cursednesse.* Cf. 423-6. The use of 'supersticious' has no implication of unreality, for the Middle Ages believed in the possibility of magic. The word, however, has a long association with diabolic art. In the seventh century, Isidore of Seville used 'superstitiosa' when he voiced the patristic condemnation of all astrology in his *Etymologiae, De Natura Rerum*, iii. 27 (ed. W. M. Lindsay, Oxford, 1911): 'Superstitious astrology is that science which is practised by the *mathematici*, who read prophecies in the heavens, and who place the twelve constellations as rulers over the members of man's body and soul and who predict the nativities and dispositions of men by the courses of the stars.' With the introduction of Greek, Jewish, and Arabic treatises into western Europe through Mohammedan Spain, and the circulation of the scientific works of Aristotle, Ptolemaeus and Albumasar, the orthodox attitude towards astrology in the twelfth century was somewhat modified. Hugh of St Victor, *Didascalion*, ii. 11 (*Pat. Lat.* 176), like Abelard and John of Salisbury, used 'superstitiosa' only of demonology. Natural astrology was approved in the thirteenth century as the science dealing with the influence of the stars upon our bodily complexions by such giants of the church as Albertus Magnus, St Thomas Aquinas, and Robert Grosseteste, though there was unanimous condem-

Notes

nation of the invocation of spirits. If the Clerk were practising only 'magyk natureel' (see 417), the Franklin's repeated invective is all the more arresting. But see Appendix IV, pp. 133-4. It might be added that Dante found a place for astrologers in his *Inferno*.

565. *tables Tolletanes*: Astronomical tables of Toledo in Spain. See Appendix IV, p. 129.

565-85. Fortunately this passage with its involved and highly technical account of the Clerk's astrological calculations need not be taken too seriously. Though Chaucer himself was a master of the subject his purpose here is artistic—to emphasize the Clerk's expertness and surround the central event of the tale with an aura of mystery. See Introduction, p. 9, and for a detailed analysis of the lines, Appendix IV, pp. 135-6.

573. The marginal gloss in El reads: *Alnath dicitur prima mansio lune.*

617. *grace*: 'unmerited favour'. Theological language was frequent in the literary convention of courtly love.

630. *the rokkes been aweye*. This declaration is the more dramatically effective after the long suspense of a speech lasting over twenty lines.

639-45. This is a stock description of grief, cf. *Anelida and Arcite*, 173, 169 (Robinson, p. 306):

Other colour then asshen hath she noon;   (cf. *FT*, 632)

She wepith, waileth, swowneth pitously. (cf. *FT*, 640-1)

646. *compleynt*. Cf. 239-40 and note.

647-8. Dorigen who before has invoked Providence, the Divine Plan, in her general questioning as to why God permits evil, now in her particular plight complains against Fortune. Fortune, a favourite goddess among the Romans, retained her popularity throughout the Middle Ages. Boethius described her activities in the *De Consolatione*. Fortune had her place in the divine plan of the universe. Providence, see note to 157, was administered through Destiny, whose influence moving further and further away from Oneness at the centre fell in ultimately with the activities of Fortune, a fickle, blind, capricious force, whose function was to govern the unstable and chequered careers of human beings in this world. All that befalls a man in this precarious existence is the gift of Fortune—whether it be riches or poverty, empire, popularity, success or disaster in love. Fortune is often represented in medieval literature, and in medieval painting and sculpture (e.g. in a wall painting on the north wall of the choir of Rochester Cathedral). She is described by Boethius and by later writers as turning a wheel which swings the men and women clinging to it to temporal prosperity, then whirls them down to utter ruin. Throughout his works Chaucer was concerned with Fortune. He wrote a series of Balades to her (Robinson, pp. 535–6). Fortune is present throughout *The Monk's Tale*, and is referred to in *The Book of the Duchess*, 617ff., *Troilus and Criseyde*, iii. 617, v. 1541–7, *Merchant's Tale*, E 2057, and *Squire's Tale*, F 577. Here Dorigen feels that she is caught and entangled in the chain attached to the wheel.

649. *For.* This reading is common to the majority of the reliable manuscripts, but it seems likely to be a scribal error for *fro*, possibly in some early exemplar.

650. This line is two syllables short of the norm not only in El but also in other good manuscripts. Artistically, the brevity serves to emphasize the tragic alternatives of this painful dilemma. Many of the manuscripts, however, read *or elles*.

652. *The compleynt of Dorigene ayeyns Fortune* is written in the margin of El.

659. *thise stories.* The following twenty-two allusions to maidens, widows, and virtuous wives are drawn entirely from St Jerome's *Adversus Jovinianum* (see chs. 41–6, *Pat. Lat.* 23, cols. 270–6). Cf. *Legend of Good Women* (Robinson, p. 490), G. 281ff. This late fourth-century treatise became one of the chief sources for the anti-matrimonial writings of the Middle Ages. To confound Jovinian's anti-ascetic affirmations, Jerome in Book I extols the value of virginity and lists the tribulations of wedlock, and, in Book II, adds supporting historical argument, illustrating how virgins and widows who refused a second marriage were honoured among Greeks, Romans, and barbarians. The Wife of Bath had based much of her reasoning on

this authority, without discriminating between Jerome's own logic and Jovinian's arguments which he repeated in order to refute them. It might be suspected that it was part of Chaucer's joke to make the Franklin draw extensively on the same work from which she had quoted, and which she had said was included in her fifth husband's favourite collection, in the manuscript which he used to read all night, to her great vexation (D 675ff.).

Extensive notes and references in Latin were copied in the margin (opposite 660–756) by the Ellesmere scribe. The majority of these occur only in the Ellesmere MS and in one other (Additional MS, 35286), though they may well have been derived from Chaucer's own additions to his original text. See below, note to 749.

660–70. The Thirty Tyrants seized power in Athens at the end of the Peloponnesian War (fifth century B.C.), and instigated a reign of terror.

679. *Aristoclides.* As the gloss states, he was a tyrant of Orchomenos in Arcadia.

680. *heet Stymphalides.* 'who was called Stymphalis'.

691. *Hasdrubales wyf.* Hasdrubal was the king of Carthage in 146 B.C. when the city was burnt by the Romans in the Third Punic War. Cf. *Nun's Priest's Tale*, B² 3362–8:

> But sovereynly dame Pertelote shrighte
> Ful louder than dide Hasdrubales wyf,
> Whan that hir housbonde hadde lost his lyf,
> And that the Romayns hadde brend Cartage.
> She was so ful of torment and of rage
> That wilfully into the fyr she sterte,
> And brende hirselven with a stedefast herte.

697. *Lucresse.* Both Livy and Ovid tell how Lucretia was raped by Tarquinius Sextus, son of Tarquinius Superbus, the last king of Rome, and killed herself rather than bring dishonour to her husband. Chaucer told the story at length in *The Legend of Good Women*, Shakespeare in *The Rape of Lucrece*.

698. *whan.* This is the reading of the majority of the best manuscripts. The line, however, has only nine syllables, and

Notes

whan that may have been in the original and omitted by error in an early exemplar.

701. *Melesie.* Miletus, southernmost of the great Ionian cities of Asia Minor, was sacked by the Gauls in 276 B.C.

706. *Habradate.* Abradates was king of the Susi. His story was told by Xenophon in *Cyropaedia*, vii. 3.

718. *Demociones.* On the death of the man to whom she had been betrothed, Demotion's daughter killed herself rather than marry another.

720. *Cedasus.* Plutarch tells the story of the daughters of Scedasus, of Leuctra in Boeotia, in his *Amatoriae Narrationes.*

724. *Nichanore.* Nicanor was one of Alexander's officers at the capture of Thebes, 336 B.C.

729. *Nicerates wyf.* When Niceratus was put to death by the Thirty Tyrants of Athens, his wife killed herself rather than fall into their hands.

731. *Alcebiades.* The Athenian general, Alcibiades, was murdered in 404 B.C. at the instigation of the Thirty Tyrants. Plutarch relates how his concubine, Timandra, in defiance of the Tyrants, buried his body.

732. The reading of El is not necessarily wrong. For the omission of an obvious pronoun, cf. 255.

734. *Alceste.* Alcestis, who died in her husband's place, was renowned in legend for her tender devotion to her husband, Admetus, king of Pherae in Thessaly. Chaucer summarized her story in *The Legend of Good Women*, F 511–16.

735. *goode Penalopee.* In the *Odyssey*, Homer related how Penelope, the faithful wife of Odysseus (Ulysses), resisted and outwitted her suitors during her husband's long absence.

737. *Laodomya.* Ovid tells her story in *Heroides*, xiii. Her husband was Protesilaus, king of Phylace in Thessaly. When he was killed at Troy by Hector, she voluntarily joined him in the underworld.

740. *noble Porcia.* Plutarch told the story of the death of Portia in his Life of Brutus, on which Shakespeare drew in

Julius Caesar. Through anxiety about her husband, she killed herself by swallowing burning coals.

743. *Arthemesie*. Artemisia showed her devotion to her husband, Mausolus, king of Caria, 352 B.C., by building a splendid sepulchre in his honour. This sepulchre was counted by the ancients as one of the seven wonders of the world. It provided the name *mausoleum* for many a magnificent tomb erected afterwards.

745. *Teuta*. She was queen of Illyria in 231 B.C. Apparently she was not married.

747-8. There is no Latin gloss to these lines which occur in only one other manuscript besides El.

747. *Bilyea*. She was the wife of Duillius, who won a naval battle against the Carthaginians in 260 B.C. She is best known for putting up with her husband's bad breath.

748. *Rodogone*. Rhodogune, the daughter of Darius, killed her nurse for trying to persuade her to a second marriage.

Valeria. She refused to marry again when she had lost her husband, Servius.

749. The preceding ninety-two lines raise several problems both of interpretation and of text. It is hard to decide how seriously this long succession of *exempla* was meant to be taken. By modern standards it is inordinately long and tedious, if taken at its face value, but it must be remembered that a wealth of illustration was favoured by the medieval rhetoricians and was according to fourteenth-century taste. The allusions when closely scrutinized are not equally pertinent, and are even inappropriate towards the end. At least twice, at 689 and 714-715, Dorigen appears to be drawing to a close. The vocabulary and tone of 669-70 and 694 are hardly suited to the dignity of the theme. It might be argued that Chaucer was demonstrating the immoderation and illogicality of a frenzied woman—after all, her enemy was the gentle Aurelius, whom she seems to be identifying with the tyrants of history. Or it might appear that Chaucer began seriously enough, and with some feeling for his theme down to the seventh example, where he grew bored, the passage got out of artistic control, the allusions became shorter and more bald, as well as less appropriate,

until they culminated in the last three names, crowded together into one unpoetical couplet, 747–8. A further possibility is that Chaucer had a purpose here other than the story—namely to ridicule a common rhetorical practice by reducing it to an absurdity.

Mrs Dempster (see Bibliography) has shown that Chaucer obviously worked here with a manuscript of *Adversus Jovinianum* before him and sifted the contents of this source at least three times to collect his examples. The suggestion of still further names in the marginal gloss of El seems to have been added by the poet himself. Acknowledgement of the source occurs at 751 in El and at 687 in at least five other manuscripts, which points to the fact that the complaint might once have ended earlier than in the present text. There is little doubt that all the lines of the complaint were written by Chaucer.

764. Cf. 'Let sleeping dogs lie.'

771. 'A pledge is the finest contract that one may keep.'

785–90. These lines occur only in El and one other manuscript.

800. *of aventure or grace*. A favourite type of alternative in Chaucer's works, cf. A 1074: 'aventure or cas'; 1465: 'aventure or destynee'; B² 4189: 'his aventure or his fortune'; E 1967: 'by destynee or aventure'—all signifying whether by chance or by some kind of intervention. Perhaps the alteration of the common phrase by the introduction of 'grace' is deliberately made to be in keeping with the Franklin, a professed son of the church (see 425–6).

825ff. The richness of Chaucer's vocabulary is partly due to his frequent selection from some 'restricted' language. Here are some of the precise idioms of medieval contractual law (cf. 869–79). Such legal diction is appropriate to the Franklin, the friend of the Man of Law, who had himself at 'sessiouns' been 'lord and sire'. At the same time the words are appropriate to Aurelius, for the legal phraseology of holding, keeping, plighting, breaking troth, etc., had become conventional clichés in the language of courtly love.

825–6. 'I surrender to you, into your keeping as discharged, every pledge . . .' The reading of El and Hg, *serement*, from Latin

Notes

sacramentum, 'oath', has been retained, though *surement*, 'security', a variant of *seuretee* (cf. 873), from Latin *securitas*, and the reading of the great majority of manuscripts, is a better parallel to 'bond'.

833-6. The majority of the manuscripts have the same order as El, but in two manuscripts these lines are placed after 842, a better position since they appear to be part of the Franklin's observations.

839. *sayd.* An unusual use of the past participle. Possibly there is a conflation of two constructions, 'heard me' and 'heard (it) said'.

871-2. '. . . however I get on, although I go abegging scantily clad in my tunic.' The use of the infinitive as an equivalent to an adverbial clause of concession was a common idiom in late Middle English. The *-ed* of *abegged* is not a past participle ending, but represents the O.E. suffix *-að. a-* is the weakened Middle English form of O.E. *on.* Cf. O.E. *on huntað*, 'ahunting'. Cf. *goon abegged, Pardoner's Prologue*, C 406: *goon ablakeberyed; Wife of Bath's Prologue*, D 354: *goon acaterwawed.*

APPENDIX I

The Poet and his Works

CHAUCER'S LIFE AND TIMES

Though Chaucer himself is for the most part silent about his personal affairs, it will be obvious from the summary of the recorded details of the external facts about the poet's life that he lived close to the centre of exciting, disturbing, and often distressing political, social and religious events. Chaucer came into contact with many of the men of importance—kings and princes, courtiers, diplomats, men of affairs and men of letters of his time. It is easy to guess what were the engrossing topics of conversation in the society among which he moved. The poet's striking reticence gives some indication of his attitude towards his art.

c. **1343**. Geoffrey Chaucer was born in London, son of John Chaucer, a prosperous wine-merchant, who was known at court and had held some public offices.

Edward III had reigned since 1327. Throughout the fourteenth century the English were fighting intermittently on two fronts—against Scotland (English defeat at Bannockburn in 1314 and victory at Neville's Cross in 1346), and against France (The Hundred Years War began about 1337. English victories at Crécy, 1346, and Poitiers, 1356, when the French king was captured.) The plague, known as the Black Death, raged in 1349 and wiped out more than a third of the population. The spirit of chivalry found expression in the institution of the Order of the Garter in 1350. The Babylonish Captivity, when the Pope was kept at Avignon in the power of the French king, lasted from 1305–78.

1357. After receiving some early education, possibly at St Paul's Cathedral School in London, Chaucer began his career as a page in the household of Elizabeth, countess of Ulster and wife of the third son of Edward III, Prince Lionel.

1359. Chaucer served with the English army in France, where he was taken prisoner. His ransom was paid in March 1360.

The English army had had the advantage in a series of harrying raids in France which terminated in the treaty of Brétigny, May 1360. The French king was ransomed, and Edward III relinquished his claim to the French throne when large provinces in France were ceded to England.

1361-7. Little is known about Chaucer's activities, but he was possibly a student at the Inner Temple during this period, and received some legal training.

The plague again raged in London in 1361 and 1362. The English were campaigning in Brittany in 1362-4, and intervening in a war in Castile in 1366-7, with disastrous results.

1367. Chaucer was in the service of the king. He was given a pension as 'dilectus valectus' and enrolled among the Esquires of the Royal Household.

1367-78. He was entrusted with several diplomatic missions, visiting France several times, Flanders in 1377, Italy 1372-3 and 1378. It is often supposed that through his travels in Italy he made the acquaintance of the works of Boccaccio, Petrarch and Dante. He appears to have been closely associated with John of Gaunt, the fifth son of Edward III. Chaucer had been married about 1366 to Philippa, a lady in the service of the queen and whose sister became the mistress and later the third wife of John of Gaunt.

1374-88. Chaucer lived in a house above Aldgate in the City of London.

1374. He was appointed Controller of Customs and Subsidies on Wools, Skins and Hides in the Port of London, an appointment which was confirmed in 1377 on the accession of Richard II. Chaucer was required to keep the accounts.

The plague was raging again in London in 1368-9. There was growing opposition to Edward III's foreign policy with its consequent heavy taxation and mounting disasters abroad. John of Gaunt made a prolonged raid in France in which he lost half his army. By 1375 only Calais was left of the English possessions in France. The king, his

Appendix I

mistress Alice Perrers, and his counsellor John of Gaunt were attacked in the Good Parliament of 1376. The Black Prince died in 1376 and Edward III in 1377. In 1378 began the Great Schism, when rival popes warred against each other. Wyclif, with the support of John of Gaunt, had begun his attack on the clergy in 1371, and by 1379 he was attacking essential Church dogma. In 1381 the people's discontent burst out in the Peasants' Revolt, during which John of Gaunt's London Palace of the Savoy was destroyed and Archbishop Sudbury murdered in the street.

1382. Chaucer was appointed Controller of the Petty Customs on wines and other merchandise, with permission to have a permanent deputy.

1385. He received the right to discharge the Controllership of Customs and Subsidies on Wools, etc., by deputy.
He became Justice of the Peace for Kent.

1386. He gave up his house in Aldgate and his employment at the Customs House, and resided in Kent, presumably at Greenwich. He was elected Knight of the Shire, i.e. Member of Parliament, but only for one year.

1389. He was appointed Clerk of the King's Works, in which position he had charge of the buildings and repairs in the Tower, Westminster Palace, and eight other royal residences, including the lodges, mews, parks, etc. Part of his duty was to see to the construction of scaffolds for tournaments and to look after walls, bridges, sewers and ditches along the Thames from Greenwich to Woolwich.

1391. He was appointed Deputy Forester of the royal forest of North Petherton in Somerset. This appointment was renewed in 1398.

1395-6. He may have been in attendance upon the son of John of Gaunt, Henry, earl of Derby (afterwards Henry IV).

In September 1399 Richard II was forced to abdicate, and Henry IV succeeded to the throne. Richard was murdered a few months later.

1399. In December Chaucer leased a house in the garden of Westminster Abbey.

1400. Chaucer died, according to his tomb in Westminster Abbey, on October 25.

The Poet and his Works

Above are the main works, but the order and the dating of many are tentative. It is likely that Chaucer often had more than one work in hand at the same time, and it is almost certain that he incorporated tales written earlier in both *The Legend of Good Women* and *The Canterbury Tales*.

Since *The Franklin's Tale* seems to be richly allusive and much of its significance grows obvious only in the wider framework of the drama of the pilgrimage, as is shown in the Introduction, it is important to consider the order of *The Canterbury Tales*, though it is impossible to be sure of the exact place of *The Franklin's Tale* in the whole series.

The order of the tales, and indeed the number, as well as the allocation of the existing connecting links, differ in various manuscripts. Manly, denying that Chaucer was responsible for any known arrangement, attributed the variation to the

---

[1] *The Equatorie of the Planetis*, ed. D. J. Price, Cambridge, 1955. Chaucer's authorship has not been definitely proved, but there is some evidence in favour of it.

Appendix I

incompleteness of the material Chaucer left and to separate attempts by several scribes to collect and arrange the tales that Chaucer was known to have written.

The connecting links with scattered references to the time of the day and to places reached on the pilgrimage suggest the following order of narrators (A B¹ B² C, etc., designate the commonly accepted groupings):

A   Knight—Miller—Reeve—Cook
B¹ Man of Law
B² Shipman—Prioress—Chaucer—Monk—Nun's Priest
D   Wife of Bath—Friar—Summoner
E   Clerk—Merchant
F   Squire—Franklin
C   Physician—Pardoner
G   Second Nun—Canon's Yeoman
H   Manciple
I   Parson

The Ellesmere MS and many other manuscripts, some in the best and oldest tradition, have: A B¹ D E F C B² G H I.

It would be supererogatory here to pursue this problem further. Both orders have been adopted by eminent scholars, and other orders suggested. It will suffice to point out that it is commonly accepted that the Knight, the Wife of Bath, the Clerk, the Merchant and the Squire preceded the Franklin.

Robinson, p. xxix, ascribed the later *Canterbury Tales* (including the 'Marriage Group') to years between 1393 and 1400. The resemblance in subject-matter and vocabulary of the astrological passages in *The Franklin's Tale* (565–71) suggests that this was written at approximately the same time as *The Equatorie of the Planetis*.

APPENDIX II

CHAUCER'S ENGLISH

Chaucer's contribution to the development of the literary language lay in his proof of the potentialities of his mother-tongue. He gave prestige and literary currency to the London dialect just at the time when that dialect was rising to supremacy above the many other dialects in England. Moreover, for three centuries Latin and French had been the prevailing languages of culture and entertainment. If Chaucer, like his contemporary Gower, had chosen first to write in Latin and French, the whole course of English literature might have been incalculably different.

The London dialect was a blend of the dialects of the neighbouring districts, chiefly east midland in character, with some south-eastern and a few south-western features. In the last decades of the fourteenth century it was at a stage of rapid transition and reconstruction—absorbing native influences which had started in the north, adopting French usage to enrich vocabulary and idiom. The inflexions of nouns and verbs were being levelled, and often in process of being lost; unstressed -*e* was fast becoming silent in final positions; stress in borrowed words was unfixed and variable. Chaucer made skilful selection from the great diversity of forms current in his day, both the old-fashioned and the new, to fulfil the requirements of his rhyme and metre.

Midway in time between the Old English period and today, Chaucer's poetry retains many traces of the Old English language, yet there is comparatively little in Chaucer's vocabulary, grammar, and syntax that will not easily be recognized by the modern reader. In his language may be discerned the first important stage in the emergence of modern standard English.

Appendix II

VOCABULARY

Chaucer's life brought him into contact with all classes of men. His own language is essentially the cultivated tongue of the best London society of his day, but it also contains echoes of the common speech of workaday England. The verbal style of *The Franklin's Tale* is refined, having far-reaching associations with literary, legal, and philosophical terminology, and repeating the conventional diction of courtly love as well as the scientific jargon of astrological magic. It has also the freshness and directness that is possible in the use of a language newly serving the purpose of literary art and not yet worn to triteness, as in *skipte adoun into the fyr* (694–5), *were cropen out of the ground* (906), *levere ystiked for to be* (768).

In his fusion of French and English words (roughly one-third of his vocabulary is of French origin), Chaucer was furthering the enrichment of a language impoverished by a long period of literary disuse. He introduced not only a great number of abstract terms but also phrases shaped according to French idiom: e.g. *bycause* (8); *by possibilitee* (635); *for me* (378); *doon his diligence* (550); *fille in tretee* (511); *swich a pitee caught* (32); and so throughout.

Comparatively little of Chaucer's vocabulary is now entirely obsolete. Most of his words are still recognizable, even when they appear in an early spelling (e.g. *arwe*, arrow; *dawes*, days; *wowke*, week), or in a French form (e.g. *accordaunt*, *defaute*, *aventure*, *avantage*, *dette*, *doute*, etc.). But there is need for vigilance where meaning is concerned. In *The Franklin's Tale* some of the technicality is obscured by its being expressed in common words which have also a highly specialized meaning. See Glossary and Notes for *argumentz*, *equacions*, *expans*, *face*, *herberwe*, *opposicioun*, *layes*, etc. Differences in sense are in fact much more frequent than the unwary reader may suspect. The context will reveal that such words as *complexioun*, temperament; *doom*, judgment; *franchise*, nobility of mind; *parcel*, part; *thriftily*, politely, are different in meaning from the common modern words to which they have a formal similarity. Usually, however, the difference is more subtly concealed. So *chalange* (616) is the equivalent of claim, *ryver* (488) a hawking ground on the bank of a river, *supersticious* (564) pertaining to diabolic art, *curiously* (201) elaborately, *fre* (914) generous, *gentil* (1) worthy, *namely* (31) especially. *lust* (104), *rage* (128), *shove* (573) have not their modern associations of carnal desire, anger, and violent pushing. *servant, servage, complayne, peyne, penaunce, obeysaunce,* etc., must be interpreted within the convention of courtly love. Sometimes, in fact, the resemblance in form is completely misleading—e.g. *wisly* (81) is an adverb derived from the Old English adjective *gewiss,* certain; *him thoughte* is the preterite of the impersonal verb, O.E. *þyncan,* to seem, and not of O.E. *þencan,* to think. *Shall, sholde, wil, wolde, kan, koude* have often a different force and meaning from those of today.

Pitfalls are everywhere, and it is advisable to consult the Glossary constantly.

SPELLING AND PRONUNCIATION

We can never hope to recapture the exact sounds of Chaucer's speech. The conventional guide given below is only an approximation, which to Chaucer would probably seem something like an attempt by an earnest foreigner. Nevertheless its application will lead to a truer and livelier impression of the music of Chaucer's poetry than any modernization can give.

The spelling of El is fairly consistent and roughly phonetic, i.e. each letter usually has some sound value. Long *a, e, o* are indicated either by a digraph as in *maad, heed, stoon,* or by a final *-e* after a single consonant, *blake, seke,* etc. Long *u* is represented by the alternatives *ou, ow,* as in *houndes, how. i* and *y* in medial position are equivalent. *-ai (-ay)* and *-ei (-ey)* are interchangeable. *o* is written for *u* in the neighbourhood of *m, n, v, w,* as in *som, songe, love, world,* to facilitate the reading of the manuscript.

Stressed Vowels

Short

a, e, i (y), o are pronounced as in French *patte,* English *pet, pit, pot.*

u (o=u) has the sound of the vowel in *put.*

Long

a, i (y), u are pronounced as in *father, ravine, rude.*

e and *o* present some difficulty owing to their varied origins. *e* sometimes has the open sound of *air,* as in *ese, heed, grete,*

sometimes the close sound of French *été* in *he, leeve* ('dear'),
seke, slepe, nedes. Modern spelling will give some guidance to
this distinction. Chaucer's words with the open sound tend to
have *ea* today, as in *ease, head, great*, while those with the close
sound tend to have *ee, ie* in modern spelling, as in *need, sleep,
lief*.

o similarly has the open sound found in modern *ore* in *oon,
stoon*, and the close sound of French *chose* in *do, good, moon*.
Modern English sometimes has *oa* in words with the open sound
as in *boat*, and often has *oo* in words with the close sound in
Chaucer's pronunciation.

u in words of French origin such as *aventure, fortune, vertu,*
retains the vowel sound of French *tu*.

Unstressed Vowels

e has the dull vowel sound found in modern *a, the*.

Its syllabic value in final position in Chaucer's poetry is
disputed. It is widely accepted that it was silent in ordinary
speech by the end of the fourteenth century. On the other hand
such rhymes as *yowthe: allowe the* (Link, F 675–6) indicate that it
could be sounded in poetry. It is safe only to say that it may, but
need not always, be sounded in *The Franklin's Tale*. It was
usually silent in the pronominal forms *hire, oure, hise, whiche*,
etc., in the present participle ending *-ynge*, in the auxiliary
verbs *dide, moste, sholde, koude, hadde, were*, etc., and in the ad-
verbs *heer(e), theer(e), thanne*.

Final *e* is often to be elided before a vowel, a French word
beginning with *h*, or a native word with a lightly stressed
initial *h* (as in *he, his, hir, hem, hadde*, etc.). Cf. El *th'orisonte* (309),
thilke (180).

Its value is more uncertain before the caesura and at the end
of the line, and before consonants in forms where the final *e*
has grammatical value, e.g. in the weak and plural forms of
the adjectives (see below), in adverbial forms such as *faste* (139),
soore (298), and in the various inflexions of the verb (see below).
From the obvious rhythm of many a line the ear will gain a
more delicate perception of the value of an unstressed *e* than
any dogmatic generalization here could give.

-en, -es are usually syllabic.

Medial *e* is sounded in trisyllabic words: e.g. *bugle-horn* (545), *Engelond* (102), *neighebour* (253). In *hevene, everych, evere, nevere*, the medial *e* is slurred.

The *-ed* ending of the preterite and past participle of weak verbs is variable, e.g. it is fully syllabic in *semed* (438), *called* (21), *dwelled* (105), but not in *cleped* (100, 102). Cf. also *maked* (206), *maad* (195).

-i- is given syllabic value in *pacient, complexioun, constellacioun*, etc.

o is elided in *t'escape* (649), *t'areste* (662), and probably elsewhere before a vowel.

Diphthongs

ai (ay), ei (ey) in *fair, vitaille, way, wey*, etc., probably have a sound midway between those in modern *lake* and *like*.

au (aw) approximates to the sound in *house. au* in words of French origin, however, e.g. *dauncen, straunge*, is pronounced as in modern *paunch*.

ew in *newe, trewe, knew*, is pronounced as in modern *few*, i.e. as a combination of *i* and *u*, while *fewe* and *lewed* have a combination of *e* and *u*.

ow, ou in *knowen, thoughte*, are pronounced as a combination of *o* and *u*, similar to the diphthong in modern *know*.

Consonants

All consonants are to be sounded, except *h* in initial position in such words of French origin as *honour, humble, humblesse*.

In *knyt, knowe, knowes, wrapped, wrecche, wreye*, both initial consonants should be heard.

Modern pronunciation will be a guide to the sounds of most of the other consonants.

In the conservative pronunciation which Chaucer is thought to have used, *gh* in *knight, bright* would sound like *-ch* in German *ich, sicher*, and in *thoughte* like *-ch* in German *ach*.

l is probably to be pronounced before *k* in *folk*.

ng is probably pronounced as in modern *longer*.

r is trilled, and always sounded, whether in medial position before other consonants or in final position.

Appendix II

Nouns

O.E. inflexional endings, which were almost as varied as those of the Latin declensions, have been generally levelled to *-es* for the genitive singular and for all cases of the plural.

Survivals of uninflected plurals occur in *folk* (248), *deer* (487), *fadme* (352), *pound* (often), *yeer* (232).

The O.E. weak plural ending *-an* is retained as *-en* in *eyen* (150). *children* (694) and *doghtren* (721; cf. *doghtres* 662) have acquired a weak plural ending.

Polysyllabic words of French origin have *-s* in the plural, *-z* where the singular ends in *-t*, e.g. *instrumentz* (4).

Adjectives

The adjective, which was to lose all trace of inflexion in the fifteenth century, is still partly inflected in Chaucer's poetry. Adjectives of native origin (except those ending in *-y*, *-ly*, *-ful*, *-ed*) end in *e* in all cases of the plural.

The O.E. 'weak' form, reduced to *-e*, is still found after demonstrative and possessive adjectives, in the vocative case, e.g. *Leeve* (899), *Eterne* (157), and before proper names (including God), e.g. *heighe* (281), *goode* (735).

The French plural ending *-s*, *-z*, is occasionally to be found in French adjectives, e.g. *delitables* (191; cf. also 565, 570).

Pronouns

Personal

The forms of the second person singular, nom. *thou*, acc. and dat. *thee*, gen. *thine*, are distinct from those of the plural, *ye*, *yow*, *youre*. The plural form is used for the singular in formal language and as a sign of respect to a superior. This distinction, however, is not always maintained. Dorigen addressing 'Eterne God' and Aurelius Apollo both mix their pronouns (e.g. 159, 172; 325, 333).

The forms of the third person plural are *they*, *hem*, *here*, *hir*. *they* is of Norse origin.

Reflexive

-self and *-selven* are used interchangeably (cf. 644, 689). The personal pronoun is often used reflexively, e.g. *romen hire* (135; cf. 141, 197, 612, 613).

116

Chaucer's English

Relative
that is the most common for all genders, singular and plural. *which(e)*, *(the) which(e) that*, are also found for both persons and things.

Indefinite
looke who that, 'whoever' (63).

Impersonal
men appears to be a survival from O.E. impersonal *man* in 83, 122, etc.

Verbs
Chaucer selected from the diverse forms current in fourteenth-century London English according to the requirements of his metre and rhyme.

Infinitive
The O.E. ending, *-an*, is sometimes preserved as *-en*, sometimes reduced to *-e*. The simple infinitive, the infinitive with *to*, and that with *for to* are used with no apparent distinction, e.g. after *hadde levere*: *dye* (888), *for to be* (768); after *gan: wepen* (754), *to swere* (81). Cf. also 605, 891; 810, 504, etc.

Present Participle
This ends in *-ynge*.

Past Participle
The O.E. past participle of strong verbs had the suffix *-en*, and a prefix *ge-*. The suffix survives as *-(e)n* or *-e*; the prefix either survives as *y-*, or has disappeared. Chaucer uses five different types, e.g. *ysworn* (330), *comen* (381), *sworn* (756), *yknowe* (179), *take* (84).

Indicative
In the *Present* the regular endings of the first, second, and third person singular are respectively *-e*, *-est*, *-eth*. The plural forms end in *-e(n)*, the characteristic ending of the east midland dialect, e.g. *pleye* (197), *pleyen* (192). Contracted forms of the third person singular are *sit* (544), *stant* (546), *lith* (629), *comth* (57).

In the *Imperative* the singular has no ending. The plural, often used politely when a single person is addressed, ends in *-eth* or *-e*. Cf. *preieth* (351), *preye* (358), *prey* (sg.) (365).

Appendix II

In the *Preterite* the O.E. plural ending, *–on*, usually appears as *–e*, occasionally as *–en*. The O.E. distinction, later often lost, is usually retained between the singular and the plural forms of strong verbs. Cf. *saugh* (480), *seigh* (142), *say* (416), with the plural *sawe* (133, 187); *gan* (sg., 428), *gonne* (pl., 210); *cam* (sg., 752), *coome* (pl., 304); etc.

highte (791), *heet* (680), 'was called', are relics of an old passive form.

Subjunctive

The singular of the present and preterite ends in *–e*, the plural in *–e(n)*. Many forms, such as *hadde, dide,* cannot be distinguished from the indicative.

For the forms of the verbs *be, have, kan, may, moot, shall, will,* see Glossary.

SYNTAX

Since the eighteenth century syntax has been regularized. Chaucer enjoyed a freedom unacceptable in modern English. Yet the syntax of *The Franklin's Tale* will present few difficulties. Conditioned though it is by the needs of the metre, the narrative has the ease, the emphasis, and the inconsistencies of informal conversation—a style suitable for a poem composed and intended for oral delivery.

It is unnecessary to analyse fully a syntax remarkably close to that of modern colloquial English. A few outstanding divergences, however, are worthy of mention.

Differences in word-order are the most obvious. A question is asked by inversion of verb and subject, e.g. *Se ye . . .?* (168), *Sey ye . . .?* (272). A command is similarly given, e.g. *Chese he . . .,* 'let him choose' (378). Inversion of subject and verb is much more common than it is today. It occurs after an emphatic adverb (e.g. *elles, nevere, now, so, thanne, tho, thus, yet*) or adverbial phrase in initial position, or when preceded by emphasized object, e.g. *Colours ne knowe I none* (15).

The object shifts its position in Chaucer's poetry, usually according to the logical stress or the needs of the versification. It intervenes in every possible place between subject and verb as well as occupying its present position, e.g. *I yow biseche* (9), *he hath his tyme yfounde* (562), *that freendes everych oother moot obeye*

(54), *if I sooth seyen shal* (62). It precedes an infinitive in *hire to disporte* (141; cf. 175, 504).

The epithet usually precedes the noun, as in modern English. Some French adjectives follow the noun, as in *magyk natureel* (417; cf. 565, 570). The post-position of a native adjective is comparatively rare (404, 483, 863), hence the repeated *blake* as the rhyme word in 151, 160, 183 is all the more arresting.

Chaucer uses a wider variety of constructions to express a negation than is possible in modern English. He often prefers a positive verbal construction with one of the following: the adjective *no (noon)* as in *Is ther no ship . . .?* (146); the adverbs *nevere, nothyng* as in *I failled nevere* (869), *nothyng list hym* (386). He negates the verb itself by adding *nat* as in *se ye nat . . .?* (168), *is nat worth* (424), or the simple negative particle *ne* as in *she ne saugh hym* (213) or in the contracted verbs *nere = ne were* (606), *nas = ne was* (632), *nyste = ne wyste* (320). For emphasis, and this occurs mainly in direct speech, the above negators are used cumulatively in varied combinations: *nevere . . . ne . . . no* (38–9); *ne nevere . . . ne* (907); *ne . . . nevere* (276); *nevere . . . ne* (845); *nevere . . . no . . . ne . . . no* (774–7); *nevere . . . no(on)* (480, 829–30); *ne . . . ne* (166); *no . . . ne* (685); *noght . . . no* (389). It was many centuries before two negatives together were to signify an affirmative.

Chaucer omits more than would be acceptable today. He omits a pronoun where it is obvious, as *she* (255), or unimportant, as *it* used in anticipation in *of Laodomya is writen* (737) or as the subject of an impersonal verb, *lothest were*, 'it would be most hateful' (605). A verb of motion is omitted in 797, and possibly *is* in *This al and som* (898).

On the other hand there are redundancies. A superfluous pronoun sometimes emphasizes the subject as in 72, 669, 675, etc., or repeats the object, e.g. 44, 521. *As* is pleonastic in *where as*, 'where' (142), *as now*, 'now' (269), and where it introduces an imperative as in 181, 351.

There is only occasional lack of concord. A singular verb follows a plural subject in 97. *hym lyked* (442) refers back to *tregetours* (435). A nominative follows the preposition *but*, 'except', in *but they thre* (500). A singular is found where modern idiom would have a partitive genitive plural in *oon of the beste farynge man* (224).

Appendix II

The syntax of the verb differs most from modern usage. There is widespread inconsistency in the use of tenses as the narrative shifts from past to present, and back again, e.g. 589–99, 384–90. The perfect tense with *have* and a past participle is often used where a simple preterite would be preferred today, and vice versa, e.g. 32, 79–80, 125; 11. Intransitive verbs are conjugated with the verb *to be*, e.g. *is goon* (313).

Impersonal constructions are very common, usually followed by some form of the infinitive, but sometimes by a *that* clause, e.g. *bihoveth me* (651); *hym fil* (409); *it happed* (252); *hem lakked* (478); *were hym levere* (814); *hym lyked* (442); *list hym* (386); *looth hym was* (811); *nedeth* (758); *hym semed* (315); *hym thoughte* (493), etc.

The infinitive is widely used. In addition to modern constructions, the infinitive is often found where Modern English would have an *–ing* form: after a verb of 'hindering' in 286; as an adjunct to a noun in 462, 678, 688; as an equivalent to a clause of supposition in 295–6, 513. The active form has a passive sense in 662–3. In *to goon a-begged* (872) it is used concessively.

Constructions of *gan, do, go*, with an infinitive deserve attention. *Gan* is to be variously interpreted. Sometimes it is redundant and untranslatable, e.g. 81; often it expresses inchoative aspect = 'began and went on', e.g. *gan to daunce* (428), *gan aswage* (127). *Do* has a causal sense = 'make', e.g. *do me lyve or deye* (629), *do myn herte breste* (348). *Go* is used with the simple infinitive in *go we soupe*, 'let us have supper' (509). A periphrastic infinitive occurs in 296, *for to go love*, 'to love'.

The subjunctive was still in living use in the fourteenth century. In principal clauses there is frequent use of the optative, e.g. 181, 666, 762, 767. The jussive subjunctive occurs in *Chese he* (378), the future conditional, = 'would be', in *this were an impossible* (301; cf. 454, 821, 875). In subordinate clauses the subjunctive is used after verbs of 'praying', 'commanding', etc., in 359, 773–5; to express future conclusion after *er, til*, e.g. 25, 51, 123; to express future condition, 331–2, 763, 889; impossible condition, 521, 606, 846; in adverbial clauses of concession, e.g. 170, 339; and of result, 352.

APPENDIX III

VERSIFICATION

The Franklin's Tale should be read aloud. Chaucer, composing originally for an audience, intended the sound of his lines to contribute to their meaning and effect. With any poem we can never be sure of wholly recapturing the intended stresses and intonations. With Chaucer's verse there is the added difficulty of fourteenth-century pronunciation, and the uncertainty of the value of final unstressed *-e* (see Appendix II). Notwithstanding these limitations, it is still true that for us not to hear the tale, even imperfectly, would be to miss a considerable part of its content.

A few general directions will give some guidance. *The Franklin's Tale*, like the *General Prologue* and most of *The Canterbury Tales* which are in verse, is written in rhymed couplets, with lines usually of ten (or eleven) syllables and a fairly regular alternation of unstressed (×) and stressed ($\underline{\,\diagup\,}$) syllables: e.g.

$$\times \quad \underline{\,\diagup\,} \quad \times \quad \underline{\,\diagup\,} \qquad \times \quad \underline{\,\diagup\,} \times \quad \underline{\,\diagup\,} \times \quad \underline{\,\diagup\,}$$
Whan maistrie comth, the god of love anon (57)

While the metrical units, viz. the couplet and the line, are firmly maintained, the sense is by no means confined by the form. The narrative flows on as sentences end mid-line (e.g. 856), extend beyond the couplet, or even start a new paragraph between the two end-rhymes (e.g. 304). The line must obviously be heard in relation with those adjoining. In fact the sentence structure often provides a counter-pattern to the line structure (e.g. 160–4).

There are a sufficient number of lines in *The Franklin's Tale* with this five-stressed pattern to establish it as the basic rhythm. But we may be sure that Chaucer did not violate the normal accentuation of the spoken word or phrase. Superimposed on the basic rhythm is the rhetorical pattern with the logical stresses and flexibility of ordinary speech. Anyone who stresses according to sense will find that the satisfaction afforded by the frequent coincidence of basic and rhetorical patterns is intensified by the subtle variations which everywhere prevent the verse from becoming mechanical.

The inner structure of the line is of great importance. Among the predominating rising measures ($\times \underline{\angle}$), various other combinations (such as $\underline{\angle} \times$, $\times \times \underline{\angle}$, $\underline{\angle} \times \times$, etc.) are deftly introduced. A favourite inversion in the beginning of a line, $\underline{\angle} \times$, repeatedly adds emphasis, or indicates a new turn of thought, e.g.

> Love wol nat been   (56), cf. 12, 29, 67, 168, etc.

> Now wol I stynten   (106), cf. 252, 284, 361, 378, etc.

As one might expect, the rhythms are the most varied in the many dialogues and monologues: e.g.

> 'Hastow nat had thy lady as thee liketh?'
> 'No, no,' quod he, and sorwefully he siketh.
> 'What was the cause? Tel me if thou kan.'
> Aurelius his tale anon bigan.   (881–4)

Much of the spontaneity and fluidity of *The Franklin's Tale* must be ascribed to the skilful introduction of a pause which ranges from the emphatic to the barely perceptible. It occurs with great regularity after the fourth or fifth syllable in the line, but it can be effectively brought forward or delayed: e.g.

> But, Lord, thise grisly feendly rokkes blake   (160)

> And lat this flood endure yeres tweyne   (354)

It can be doubled:

> She seyde: 'Sire, sith of youre gentillesse'   (46)

or further multiplied most impressively:

> Yong, strong, right vertuous, and riche, & wys.
> (225, cf. 240)

Its omission, coupled with enjambement, and inverted stress, evokes the sensation of the continuous sinking it describes in

Versification

> Prey hire to synken every rok adoun
> Into hir owene dirke regioun
> Under the ground, ther Pluto dwelleth inne.   (365–7)

Variations of pause and stress within the line can similarly underline the sense. The smooth description of Aurelius's realization that:

> ther was noon obstacle,
> That voyded were thise rokkes everychon   (592–3)

is in striking contrast to the lines implying the difficulties of the feat

> that alle the rokkes blake
> Of Britaigne weren yvoyded everichon.   (450–1)

An intent listener may discover the suggestion of the constant renewal of light in *Thanne shal she been evene atte fulle alway* (361), and of the continuance of the tide in *And spryng flood laste . . .* (362). The impact of the encounter is conveyed by *A yong clerk romynge by hymself they mette* (465), Aurelius's steady advance is contained in

> and forth, moore and moore,
> Unto this purpos drough Aurelius.   (256–7)

The stresses have not necessarily equal force. Pronouns, auxiliary verbs, prepositions, conjunctions, do not usually bear stress, and a line composed with some of these may have fewer stresses than the normal five. The only real stresses in a line are the logical stresses. These lighter lines, too, can be very appropriate: e.g.

> Wolde han maked any herte lighte.   (206)

> In hope for to been lissed of his care.   (462)

The rhymes also help to prevent any mechanical monotony by their mixed appeal of satisfied expectation and surprise. Chaucer had a good ear for the exact rhyme, which generally falls into its place without any strain. He had a wide choice: masculine rhymes (ending with the stressed syllable) are placed among feminine rhymes (two-syllabled, with the final syllable unstressed) in roughly equal proportion. Many of his

123

Appendix III

rhymes are two-syllabled: e.g. masculine rhyme *confus-ioun*:
creac-ioun (161-2); feminine rhymes *dayes*: *layes* (1-2); *destroyen*:
anoyen (175-6). Often two words balance one: *anon*: *is gon*
(57-8); *in love*: *above* (63-4); *wight is*: *amys* (71-2). Often a
suffix and a full word are ingeniously linked: e.g. *and a stable*:
unresonable (163-4); *delitables*: *ches and tables* (191-2). Sometimes
the rhyme is limited to the last syllable: *Venus*: *Aurelius* (229-
230); *lat-oun*: *declynaci-oun* (537-8). Only occasionally is it con-
fined to the same suffix: *curiously*: *trewely* (201-2); *mariage*:
servage (85-6).

To fulfil the requirements of his versification Chaucer made
deft use of the vairations in late fourteenth-century London
English, using forms old and new (see Appendix II).

The stress in words of French origin was variable. Usually
Chaucer retains the original stress on the final syllable, e.g.
matér (239), *honóur* (254), *manére* (363), *tretée* (511), *citée* (463),
etc. He also took advantage of the English tendency to stress
the first syllable when his line needed it. And so:

sérvant (84), ?*servánt* (85), *serváge* (86); *vítaille* (196), *vitaílle* (478,
910); *rýveres* (346), *ryvér* (488); *sóper* (504), *sopér* (502); *pítee*
(723), *pitée* (895); *mádame* (615), *madáme* (623), etc.

APPENDIX IV

Astronomy, Astrology, and Magic

The following discussion of six 'scientific' allusions (viz. 73–5, 323–7, 349–50, 417–23, 537–40, 554–82) in their context of medieval thought will prove to be more central than at first it may appear. Though this appendix seems to range widely from the story of the problems of the four chief characters of *The Franklin's Tale*, it ought not to be forgotten that Chaucer conceived the fortunes of his creatures against a medieval background and that the significance of his plot was understood by his audience in the light of contemporary beliefs. It is a truism to add that any close consideration of Chaucer's usage might be expected to repay effort by revealing the subtlety of the poet's art.

The Structure of the Universe

From ancient days and until the seventeenth century, cosmology assumed a geocentric system—the earth, a solid sphere, fixed and motionless at the centre of the universe. To explain day and night, the cycle of the seasons, the changing positions of the planets and stars in the sky, all the heavenly bodies were held to be revolving round the earth. As early as c. 370 B.C. Eudoxus had postulated the system of concentric spheres which was adopted by Aristotle, from whom it took its name. The Aristotelian system was popularly accepted in the Middle Ages, after the Arabic treatises which had preserved it had been translated into Latin. The Church favoured an explanation of the architecture of the universe which clearly demonstrated the unity of all creation. The system readily lent itself to poetic treatment—Dante based *The Divine Comedy* upon it; Chaucer described it at the end of *Troilus and Criseyde*, Milton in *Paradise Lost*.

Though there were many variations in detail, fundamentally the descriptions of the Aristotelian system are the same. The universe was believed to consist of a series of concentric hollow spheres, one within the other like the skins of an onion, round the earth at the centre. Attached one to each sphere, and in the order of their increasing distance from the earth, were the seven planets—Moon, Mercury, Venus, Sun, Mars, Jupiter, Saturn. The eighth sphere around these contained the stars. The whole was held within the ninth sphere, which was known as the Primum Mobile. It was disputed whether the spheres were solid, but certainly they were transparent and invisible: all that could be seen from earth were their attached planets and stars.

ASTRONOMY

The Motions of the Heavenly Bodies

According to medieval theory the nine spheres all revolved round the motionless earth. The heavenly poles lay immediately above the north and south poles of the earth, the heavenly equator above the equator on earth's surface. The outermost sphere, the Primum Mobile, rotating from east to west round the axis of the heavenly poles, completed its revolution of 360° round the earth every twenty-four hours. Being all-powerful, it carried round with it the eight spheres within it, causing the alternation of day and night. Each of the other spheres had its own motion, independent of the rest. Greek astronomers had observed that the planets moved, each independently, in orbits considerably inclined to the direction of the daily rotation, and they maintained that the movement of each planet was from west to east, i.e. contrary to the daily rotation. The planets moved at different rates. The moon was carried west to east round the earth in approximately 28 days, Mercury, Venus and the sun in approximately 365 days, Mars in $2\frac{1}{2}$ years, Jupiter in 12 years, Saturn in 30 years. The planets all made further revolutions within their own spheres, but not the stars in the eighth sphere, which were therefore called 'fixed'. The stars moved only with the sphere itself, which, to account for the precession of the equinoxes,[1] was calculated to be making a

[1] i.e. the gradual westward shift of the equinoctial points along the path of the sun, the ecliptic. Each year the sun is less advanced on its apparent path through the belt of the zodiac than it was at the same time the year before.

very slow revolution from west to east which took 3600 years
to complete.

Coexistent from early times with this hypothesis of concen-
tric spheres was what is known as the Ptolemaic system of
measurement by means of eccentric circles and epicycles.
Claudius Ptolemy in the second century A.D. in his *Syntaxis*
(Arabic *Almagest*) had elaborated a system of computation to
explain such apparent irregularities in the planetary motions
as were unaccounted for by the theory of concentric spheres.
When closely observed from earth, some of the planets were
seen to be moving not at a uniform rate, but sometimes going
faster, sometimes more slowly, or even moving backward,
obviously at times nearer to earth than at other times. The
motion of the moon as seen from earth, for example, has been
compared to that of a lighted torch held at arm's length by a
man who continually revolved while running round a circular
track, as it would be seen by one, standing near but not at the
centre of the track, on a dark night when only the torch would
be visible. To state this in Ptolemaic terminology: the moon
was described as revolving at a uniform rate in a circle
(*epicycle*), whose centre moved regularly at a uniform rate
round another circle (*deferent*), and the deferent circle itself was
eccentric, i.e. its centre was not coincident with the centre of
the earth, and therefore with the centre of the universe. This
system of eccentric circles and epicycles, modified to account
for other planets, enabled astronomers to determine the position
of any planet at any time with an accuracy amazing, even when
compared with modern calculations.

The Measurement of the Positions of the Heavenly Bodies

Central to all the kinds of measurements invented by the
ancient astronomers is that of the circular belt of the zodiac
(from Greek *zoon*, 'animal', cf. names of the signs). The annual
orbit of the sun, the ecliptic, was discovered to intersect the
plane of the celestial equator in two opposite points at an angle
of $23\frac{1}{2}°$, so that half of the sun's path is north and half south of
the equator. As the sky is seen from the earth, all the planets
were found to move within a belt $12°$ wide, lying equally on
either side of the ecliptic. This belt was divided into twelve
equal areas, each one named after that constellation in the

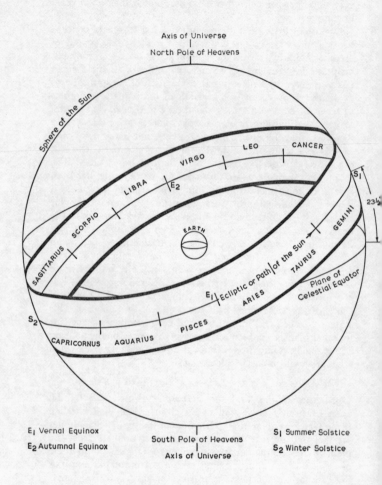

Axis of Universe
North Pole of Heavens

Sphere of the Sun

CANCER
LEO
VIRGO
LIBRA
E₂
SCORPIO
SAGITTARIUS

S₁
23½°

GEMINI
TAURUS
Ecliptic or Path of the Sun
EARTH
E₁
ARIES
Plane of
Celestial Equator

S₂
CAPRICORNUS   AQUARIUS   PISCES

E₁ Vernal Equinox
E₂ Autumnal Equinox

South Pole of Heavens
Axis of Universe

S₁ Summer Solstice
S₂ Winter Solstice

128

eighth sphere which, to those on earth, originally appeared to lie within it. The divisions, or signs, of the zodiac are, in order: Aries (Ram), Taurus (Bull), Gemini (Twins), Cancer (Crab), Leo (Lion), Virgo (Virgin), Libra (Scales), Scorpio (Scorpion), Sagittarius (Archer), Capricornus (Goat), Aquarius (Water-carrier), Pisces (Fishes). Each sign occupied 30° of the zodiac. For closer accuracy of description each sign was further divided into three equal parts of 10° each, called 'faces', and five un-equal parts, called 'terms'. The first sign, Aries, was reckoned from the point where the ecliptic intersected the plane of the celestial equator. This was at the period of equal day and night, the spring equinox, by a faulty calculation made March 12 instead of March 21 in the Middle Ages. The other signs followed, anti-clockwise, in the order given above. At the summer solstice, the sun in the northern hemisphere was entering the sign of Cancer, at the autumn equinox Libra, at the winter solstice Capricorn. Because of the inclined path of the sun west to east, and the diurnal rotation of the universe east to west, the sun's course appears from earth to be a spiral, rising higher towards the north pole each day from midwinter to midsummer, and then descending again. The 'declinacioun' (325–7, 538) refers to the celestial latitude of the sun, the angular distance of the sun in the sky reckoned from the plane of the equator. In the northern hemisphere the declination is greatest at the summer solstice when the sun is in the sign of Cancer, and least in the winter solstice, in the sign of Capricorn. Chaucer uses this measurement to refer to the change of the seasons and the effect of the summer or winter sun on vegetation.

The calculations of the moving positions of the heavenly bodies were helped in the Middle Ages by complicated instruments like the Equatorium for planets and the Astrolabe for the stars (both described in works written by Chaucer, see Appendix I), and by astronomical tables. Such tables were numerous, but the most widely used were the Alfonsine Tables, drawn up for Toledo, c. 1272, under the patronage of Alfonso X (the Wise), king of Leon and Castile (1252–84), probably the Clerk's 'tables Tolletanes' (565). The Alfonsine Tables correc-ted and superseded earlier tenth-century Toledo tables, and were themselves later adapted to fit the longitude of Paris, Oxford, and London, as extant manuscripts prove. The main body of these tables gives information of general validity, constants, of which two of the most important are the two angles, the mean motus and the mean argument, the former governing position in the eccentric circle, the latter in the epicycle. Since these angles increase at a uniform rate with time, they could be tabulated. The 'root' (568) is the first date for which the table is given, often the Birth of Christ. Tables of motions for 'collect' years (567) showed the number of signs, degrees, minutes, and seconds, to be added to the datum of the root for the reckoning of the motion of the planet during long periods of time—in round numbers, such as 100, 200, 500, 1000 years. A table of 'expans yeeres' (567) showed the computation necessary to allow for changes in position during short periods, which could bring the calculation up to the beginning of the year in question. Previous editors have assumed that the 'proporcioneles convenientz' (570) is Chaucer's name for tables giving the planet's movement during a fraction of a year.

It would be inappropriate here, even were it possible, to attempt to follow all the calculations that the Clerk might be assumed to have made, to determine when the moon would be in the exact position most propitious for his undertaking. It would be profitable, however, to glance at the pages of *The Equatorie of the Planetis*. Though the computations there may not be understood, it will be readily apparent that this treatise abounds in the kind of jargon which the Franklin uses. There are Alfonsine Tables, roots, centres (cf. 569)—centre earth, centres deferent of eccentric circles, centres of epicycles—arguments mean and true (cf. 569), equations of the centre, equations of the argument (cf. 571). The astrologer in *The Franklin's Tale* was evidently applying his knowledge of the Ptolemaic System to the task in hand.

ASTROLOGY

It was of paramount importance to be able to ascertain the position of the planets and the stars because the Middle Ages believed that everything beneath the moon was affected by a multitude of influences proceeding from the heavenly bodies.

In fact, the word 'influence' (*lit.* 'a flowing in') came by its original sense in this way. Each subdivision of the zodiac and the segments of the heavens had their influences which modified the influence of the planets moving through them. To each of the planets were ascribed particular qualities, and the power to produce corresponding dispositions in men,[1] and to shape their characters and fortunes, either for good or bad. Each of the planets was thought to govern certain parts of the body and certain regions of the earth, and to affect certain diseases. For each planet there was at least one sign of the zodiac, called its *mansion* or *house*, in which it was supposed to exercise a particularly strong influence. When a sign was in the ascendant, i.e. to the observer on earth, just appearing above the eastern horizon—the planet whose mansion it was had special importance. If a planet was in its own sign, then as 'lord of the ascendant' its influence was most powerful. Each subdivision of the sign—the face or the term—had its own most influential planet. The Clerk

> knew the arisyng of his moone weel,
> And in whos face, and terme.   (579–80)

He would know when the moon would appear above the eastern horizon, and in which sign of the zodiac, and in which part of that sign, and to which planets these divisions belonged—in short, he knew the sum total of influences. Aurelius's knowledge was more elementary, though he was aware that the relative positions of the planets were significant. When two planets were in opposition, i.e. 180° apart according to the angle subtended between them on earth, they were very powerful. When the sun and moon were in opposition the highest tides would occur, and their power would be most strong when the sun was in its own mansion, or sign, Leo (349–50). The 'constellacioun' (73), which, like anger or strong drink, can cause one to 'doon amys or speken', refers in general terms to the influence on man through the configuration of the planets and stars.

[1] Our adjectives 'lunatic', 'jovial', 'mercurial', 'saturnine' are derived from this belief in the influence of the planets Moon (Luna), Jupiter (Jovis), Mercury, Saturn.

Appendix IV

Though the terms were interchangeable in the Middle Ages, we may understand 'Astronomy' as the science of the heavens, determining the positions and motions of the heavenly bodies, 'Astrology' as the practical application of that science to human use. An astrologer watched the heavenly bodies and made his calculations for a variety of purposes, to predict from the position of the stars and planets at the time of a man's birth his temperament or future fortune (Judicial Astrology), to foretell natural phenomena such as storms, drought, heat or floods, to choose a time suitable for some undertaking (his choice was known as 'election'), or to help him to gain some power over the elements (astrological magic). The Clerk of *The Franklin's Tale* busied himself about the last three.

MAGIC

The pivot of *The Franklin's Tale* is the apparent disappearance of the black rocks in the sea worked through magic by the occult control of natural forces. There is no question of charlatanism. The people of the Middle Ages credited magic, and 'it semed that alle the rokkes were aweye' (588). According to 581–2, the Clerk would appear to be relying upon such a book as that seen by Aurelius's brother (416–17, 421–3). Many medieval textbooks of natural magic and black magic still exist. Chaucer was probably familiar with one, though he does not give precise enough details to help in the search for it. We may guess that its contents were not unlike those in the British Museum MS Harleian 80, which combines many Ptolemaic tables with a description of the mansions of the moon and natural magic. An actual illustration of the mansions of the moon appears in at least one surviving MS, Vatican Reginensis Latinus 1283, f. 23ᵛ (see frontispiece), which is almost certainly a copy of an original belonging, like the 'tables Tolletanes' (565), to the time of Alfonso X, from whose court the influence of Arabic astrological traditions spread through Europe. It will be noted that ships and, possibly, rocks are represented in several of the mansions. If Chaucer had seen an illustration of this kind its associations may have contributed something to the poem's complex inspiration, for Dorigen's fears during her walks along the coast (142ff.) determine her conditions to

Aurelius, which are ultimately to be fulfilled through magic worked by means of the moon.

The only planet mentioned specifically in connection with the Clerk's operations is the moon. From earliest antiquity—in Chaldea, Babylon, India and Egypt—the moon had always been closely connected with magic. Being the nearest of the planets to earth, it was naturally thought to be the most influential upon it, and to collect and transmit the influences from the other planets. In all 'elections', the moon's position was of prime importance.

Through Arabic, ancient traditions concerned with the mansions of the moon were brought to Spain and Southern Italy, and so to western Europe. The traditions vary in detail, but have the same foundation—twenty-eight equal divisions of the path of the moon in a lunar month, independent of the divisions of the zodiac. A comprehensive study of the mansions of the moon has still to be written but sufficient information can be gleaned to give some idea of their significance.

Each mansion had a name, taken from part of the constellation that appeared from earth to lie within it. Alnath, the name of a star at the tip of Aries, was the Arabic name given to the first mansion. The traditions are inconsistent in their description of the influence of the different mansions. No mansion, as far as is known, is connected with the removal of rocks, or with the producing of illusions, though some are associated with water and floods, several with destruction and devastation, and many help generally in the winning of something desired.

By natural magic, the astrologer was enabled through his lore to predict from the mansions of the moon times favourable for any enterprise and to forecast such natural phenomena as storms, winds, and floods. But these same mansions readily served for the practice of black magic, worked by means of spirits. The manuscripts examined give information as to the process. First the mansion propitious to the undertaking must be found. When the moon was in that mansion an image was to be made, directions being given for the shape and the material. This image was to be inscribed with the name of the god of that mansion and sometimes with the petition. Further instructions told with what vapours the image was to be suffumigated, how the god was to be invoked, and what must finally be done with the image.

From the beginning the Church uncompromisingly denounced black magic. And so the *Speculum Astronomiae*, popularly attributed to Albertus Magnus, describing the twenty-eight images of the mansions of the moon and the fifty-four spirits who served the images and produced magic illusions, associated the twenty-eight mansions with the diabolic arts. Chaucer mentions only natural magic, but it seems possible that the Clerk worked his illusions through spirits, for—

> he clapte hise handes two,
> And farewel! al oure revel was ago. (495-6)

The ritual outlined above may well resemble the

> othere observaunces
> For swiche illusiouns and swiche meschaunces
> As hethen folk useden in thilke dayes. (583-5)

The repeatedly expressed contempt for the Clerk's practices is therefore not surprising from the Franklin, a worthy citizen and a pillar of society:

> the operaciouns
> Touchynge the eighte and twenty mansiouns
> That longen to the moone, and swich folye
> As in oure dayes is nat worth a flye—
> For Hooly Chirches feith in oure bileve
> Ne suffreth noon illusioun us to greve. (421-6)

In these lines the Franklin was probably the mouthpiece of the poet too, for despite Chaucer's wide knowledge of astronomy and astrology, when he was speaking in his own person to 'lyte Lowys, my sone' in the *Treatise on the Astrolabe*, he felt bound to add: 'Natheles these ben observaunces of judicial matere and rytes of payens, in whiche my spirit hath no feith.' (Robinson, p. 551.)

At line 558 we read

> I ne kan no termes of astrologye

and the interesting question arises: Is it possible to reconcile the Franklin's protest of ignorance with his following eighteen lines

(565–83), which are undeniably full of specimens of the correct jargon, and make some sense? One must consider the lines closely before being satisfied with the easy explanation that here is the conventional declaration of ignorance, such as Chaucer often introduced playfully before a display of knowledge.

Chaucer's lucid and precise statements in *The Astrolabe* and probably in *The Equatorie of the Planetis* leave no doubt of his own mastery of astronomy and astrology. He had deliberately transformed the stock magician of *Il Filocolo* into an astrologer. In adopting the same date for the miracle as in the Italian story he was doubtlessly aware of the astrological fitness of the early days of January. Professor Tatlock has fully demonstrated the propitiousness of the time (see Notes, 537–47). The sun would enter the last ten degrees of Capricorn on the 2nd or 3rd of January. The full moon, exactly opposite, would be in the last ten degrees of Cancer. 21°–30° Cancer are, in fact, the face of the moon, through which the full moon would pass in about three-quarters of a day on January 2 or 3. 20°–26° belong to Jupiter, according to the twelfth-century *Epitome totius Astrologiae* of Joannes Hispalensis, and Jupiter's influence is favourable to man. For some five or six degrees, in the fourth term and the third face of Cancer, the moon was at its strongest. No other time could be so propitious. It behoved the Clerk to act at once, for in less than twenty-four hours after entering this favourable term, the moon would enter the term of Saturn, 27°–30°, most inauspicious to man.

All this is left unstated. The Franklin devoted seven lines (565–71) to a list of the Clerk's equipment, appropriate but rather vague. The tables could have been 'corrected' (566) to remove errors or to allow for the precession of the equinoxes, or they could have been adapted to fit the locality. If the usual definition of *proporcioneles convenientz* is accepted, then logically these tables should follow those of the *expans yeeris*. *Rootes* appertain to *centris* and *argumentz*. But *centris, argumentz, equacions* are terms used here too imprecisely to convey more than the haziest meaning. The actual calculations begin at 572. Lines 572–4, put simply, show that the Clerk is making allowance for the slow rotation of the eighth sphere which causes the precession of the equinoxes, but this is expressed in a riddle, correct, but needlessly complicated. Alnath, the star in the eighth sphere, is at the beginning of the constellation Aries. Originally the twelve signs of the zodiac, measured sometimes in the eighth, sometimes in the ninth sphere, coincided with the constellations from which they took their names. Then, Alnath would appear at the beginning of the sign, Aries. Now that the eighth sphere had shifted somewhat, Alnath had moved away from the beginning of the sign, 'the heed of thilke fixe Aries above' (574), and the distance between would be the distance that the eighth sphere had rotated. There is a spurious link between this passage and the next, for Alnath also gave its name to the first mansion of the moon. What follows is possibly even more equivocal. What is *remenaunt* (578)? Is it the position of the other mansions, later positions of the moon, or the rest of the information he required? Lines 579–80 need further explanation if they are to have any meaning. Otherwise the reader may well wonder if the 'arisyng of his moone' refers to the period when the moon is in the ascendant, i.e. just appearing above the horizon. We are never told what phase of the moon it is: we only guess that it was the full moon. The collocation of 'face' and 'term' suggests that this is a reference to the divisions of a sign of the zodiac, but 'face' is also used of a division of the mansion of the moon. *whos* (580) might refer either to the sign or to the planets powerful in the particular 'face' and 'term' in which the moon rose. The Clerk knew also which of the moon's mansions was the most propitious, but we are not told. Neither are we told about his 'othere observaunces'.

We are clearly justified in assuming that Chaucer intended this long string of abstruse allusions to be vague and bewildering. This passage certainly does not seem to be a repetition of a favourite joke. Though we can never ascertain how much astrology the Franklin might have truly claimed to know (see Introd., 'The Franklin and his Tale'), we are sure of the poet's art. By skilfully drawing upon his own undisputed wealth of information, Chaucer has given a consistent portrait of the Franklin, and through the words of the Franklin, by the piling up of half-intelligible details, has impressed upon everyone that the particular Clerk who dominated the tale was a very subtle Clerk indeed.

SELECT BIBLIOGRAPHY

Note. Books asterisked are available in paperback editions

*Baugh, A. C., *Chaucer*, New York, 1968 (Goldentree Biblio-
graphies).

EDITIONS

The Ellesmere Chaucer (reproduced in facsimile), Manchester,
1911.
Baugh, A. C., *Chaucer's Major Poetry*, London and New York,
1963.
Donaldson, E. T., *Chaucer's Poetry*, New York, 1958.
Manly, J. M., *Canterbury Tales by Geoffrey Chaucer*, New York,
1928.
Manly, J. M. and Rickert, E., *The Text of the Canterbury Tales*,
8 vols., Chicago, 1940.
Robinson, F. N., *The Complete Works of Geoffrey Chaucer*, 2nd edn.,
London and Boston, 1957.
Skeat, W. W., *The Complete Works of Geoffrey Chaucer*, 7 vols.,
Oxford, 1894-7.
Spearing, A. C., *The Franklin's Tale*, Cambridge, 1966.

GENERAL STUDIES

A. CHAUCER AND HIS WORKS

*Bolton, W. F. (ed)., *Sphere History of Literature in the English
Language, I, The Middle Ages*, London, 1970.
Bowden, M., *A Commentary on the General Prologue to the Canter-
bury Tales*, New York, 1967.
—A Readers' Guide to Geoffrey Chaucer, New York, 1964.
*Burrow, J. A., *Geoffrey Chaucer* (Penguin Critical Anthologies),
Harmondsworth, 1969.

Bibliography

*Coghill, N., *The Poet Chaucer* (OPUS), 2nd edn., London, 1967.
*—*Geoffrey Chaucer* (Writers and Their Work, No. 79), London, 1956.
*Donaldson, E. T., *Speaking of Chaucer*, London, 1970.
*Hussey, M., with Spearing, A. C. and Winny, J., *An Introduction to Chaucer*, Cambridge, 1965.
*Hussey, S. S., *Chaucer. An Introduction*, London, 1971.
  Kean, P. M., *Chaucer and the Making of English Poetry*, 2 vols., London, 1972.
*Lawlor, J., *Chaucer*, London, 1968.
*Lowes, J. L., *Geoffrey Chaucer*, Oxford, 1934.
  Robertson, D. W., *A Preface to Chaucer*, London, 1963.
  Rowland, B., *A Companion to Chaucer Studies*, Oxford, 1968.
  Ruggiers, P. G., *The Art of the Canterbury Tales*, Wisconsin, 1967. (The section on the *Franklin's Tale* is also in Burrow, *Geoffrey Chaucer*.)
Tillotson, K., Article on Chaucer in Chamber's *Encyclopaedia*, 1955.

B. CHAUCER'S WORLD

(i) *The Fourteenth Century*

*Hussey, M., *Chaucer's World*, Cambridge, 1967.
*McKisack, M., *The Fourteenth Century, 1307–1399*, Oxford, 1959.
  Loomis, R. S., *A Mirror of Chaucer's World*, Princeton, 1965.

(ii) *Medieval Science, Astrology and Magic*

*Curry, W. C., *Chaucer and the Mediaeval Sciences*, 2nd edn., Oxford, 1960.
  Price, D. J., 'Chaucer's Astronomy', *Nature*, 170, Sept. 20, 1952.
  —*The Equatorie of the Planetis*, Cambridge, 1955.
  Sarton, G., *Introduction to the History of Science*, vol. iii, pt. 2, Carnegie Institution of Washington, 1948.
  Thorndike, L., *A History of Magic and Experimental Science*, vols. 1–4, New York, 1923–4.
  Wood, C. D., *Chaucer and the Country of the Stars*, Princeton, 1970.

Bibliography

(iii) *Literary Influences*

Donovan, M. J., *The Breton Lay*, Notre Dame and London, 1969.

*Lewis, C. S., *The Allegory of Love*, Oxford, 1936, 1959.

*Manly, J. M., 'Chaucer and the Rhetoricians', in Schoeck, R. J. and Taylor, J., *Chaucer Criticism, I, The Canterbury Tales*, Notre Dame, 1960.

Marie de France, *Lais*, ed. A. Ewart, Oxford, 1947.

*Muscatine, C., *Chaucer and the French Tradition*, Los Angeles, 1957.

Nims, M. F., trans., *The Poetria Nova of Geoffrey of Vinsauf*, Toronto, 1967.

Spearing, A. C., *Criticism and Medieval Poetry*, ch. 3, London, 1964.

SHORT STUDIES

Blenner-Hassett, R., 'Autobiographical Aspects of Chaucer's Franklyn', *Speculum*, 28, 1953.

Dempster, G., 'Chaucer at Work on the Complaint in *The Franklin's Tale*', *Modern Language Notes*, 52, 1937.

—'A Further Note on Dorigen's *Exempla*', *Modern Language Notes*, 54, 1939.

Dempster, G. and Tatlock, J. S. P., *The Franklin's Tale*, ch. xiv in Bryan, W. F. and Dempster, G., *Sources and Analogues of Chaucer's Canterbury Tales*, London, 1958.

Gaylord, A. T., 'The Promises in *The Franklin's Tale*', *Journal of English Literary History*, 21, 1964.

Golding, M. R., 'The Importance of Keeping "Trouthe" in *The Franklin's Tale*', *Medium Aevum*, 39, 1970.

Hume, K., 'Why Chaucer calls *The Franklin's Tale* a Breton Lai', *Philological Quarterly*, 51, 1972.

Kearney, A. M., 'Truth and Illusion in *The Franklin's Tale*', *Essays in Criticism*, 19, 1969. (See further vols. 20–21, 1970–1971.)

Kittredge, G. L., 'Chaucer's Discussion of Marriage', *Modern Philology*, 9 (1911–12), reprinted in Schoeck and Taylor, *Chaucer Criticism* (*see* B iii above).

Lawlor, J., '*Auctoritee* and *Pref*', ch. 6 in Lawlor, *Chaucer*.

Bibliography

Loomis, L. H., 'Chaucer and the Breton Lays of the Auchinleck Manuscript', *Studies in Philology*, 38, 1941.

—'Secular Dramatics in the Royal Palace, Paris, 1378, 1389, and Chaucer's "Tregetoures" ', *Speculum*, 33, 1958.

Lowes, J. L., 'The Franklin's Tale, Teseide, and the Filocolo', *Modern Philology*, 15, 1918.

Lumiansky, R. M., 'The Character and Performance of Chaucer's Franklin', *University of Toronto Quarterly*, 20, 1951.

Mann, L. A., 'Gentilesse and *The Franklin's Tale*', *Studies in Philology*, 63, 1966.

Sledd, J., 'Dorigen's Complaint', *Modern Philology*, 45, 1947–8.

Tatlock, J. S. P., 'Astrology and Magic in Chaucer's Franklin's Tale', *Anniversary Papers—for G. L. Kittredge*, Ginn, 1913.

—*The Scene of the Franklin's Tale Visited*, Chaucer Soc., Ser. 2, no. 51, 1914.

Tuve, R., *Seasons and Months*, Paris, 1933.

Wood, C. D., 'Of Time and Tide in the *Franklin's Tale*', *Philological Quarterly*, 45, 1966.

GLOSSARY

ABBREVIATIONS

A-begged, goon a-begged, go abegging, 872

Above, *adv.* in good fortune, 87; in addition, 447; above, in heaven, 613; **al above,** entirely in authority, 64

Abyde, *v.* endure, 215; stay, 534; **abyde fro,** abstain from, 814

Accord, *n.* agreement, 83. *See* **Fil**

Acordaunt, *adj.* appropriate, 582

Acordeth to, 3 *s.pr.* agrees with, 90

Adoun, *adv.* down, 540; **sitte adoun,** sit down, 154

After, *prep.* according to, 325;

after the tyme, in accordance with the occasion, 77. *See* **Oon**

Agayn, *adv.* **come agayn,** come back, 131; *prep.* against, 40

Agayns, *prep.* against, 637

Ago, *pp.* departed, 496

Al, *adj.* all, 104; **alle,** *pl.* 285; *adv.* just, 120; wholly, 148; quite, 508; **al be,** although it be, 622; **al be they,** although they be, 170; **al a day,** an entire day, 640; *pron.* everything, 41; **at al,** wholly, 228; **al and som,** the whole and every part, the sum of the matter, 898

Alcebiades, Alcibiades, 731

141

Glossary

Alceste, Alcestis, 734

Aleyes, *n.pl.* paths, 305

Alle, *see* Al

Allone, *adj.* alone, 211

Allowe, 1 *s.pr.* applaud, *L* 676

Alnath, *the Arabic name of a star in the constellation Aries,* 573

Als, *adv.* also, 890

Alwey, *adv.* always, 128; continuously, 212

Amonges, *prep.* among, 217

Amor(o)us, *adj.* **this amorous folk,** these people in love, 510; **amorus on,** in love with, 792

Amydde, *prep.* in the middle of, 794

Amys, *adv.* amiss, 72

An, *prep.* **an heigh,** above, 141

And, *conj.* if, 763

Angre, *n.* anger, 845

Anlaas, *n.* a short two-edged dagger, *GP* 357

Ano(o)n, *adv.* at once, 57, 518; without delay, 781; **anon right,** forthwith, 600

Anoyeth, 3 *s.pr.* injures, 167

Apayd, *adj.* pleased, 840

Apparences, *n.pl.* illusions, 432; **apparence of jogelrye,** conjuring trick, 557

Appollo, Apollo, 323

Arace, *v.* tear away, 685

Areste, *v.* **for t'areste,** to be arrested, 662

Argumentz, *n.pl.* reasoning, 178; arguments, *angles,* 569. *See Appendix IV*

Aries, Ram, *a constellation in the eighth sphere, and the name of the first sign of the zodiac,* 574

Aright, *adv.* properly, *L* 694

Aristoclides, *a tyrant of Orchomenos in Arcadia,* 679

Arisyng, *n.* ascension, rising, 579

Armes, *n.pl.* arms, 103

Armorik, Armorica, Brittany, 21

Array, *n.* dress, outfit, 219

Arrayed, *pp.* adorned, 202; ordered, 479

Arthemesie, Artemisia, 743

Artow, 2 *s.pr.* art thou, 382

Arwe, *n.* arrow, 404

As, as in, as a result of, 49; **where as,** where, 142; **as now,** now, 269; **as kepe,** may (God) keep, 181; **as preieth,** pray, 351

Assaye, *v.* attempt, 859

Asterte, *v.* escape, 314

Astoned, *pp.* stunned, 631

Aswage, *v.* diminish, 127

At, at after dyner, after dinner, 210

Atte, atte laste, at the last, 30; **atte le(e)ste,** at the very least, 456, *L* 697

Atteyne, *v.* overcome, 67

Atthenes, Athens, 661

Aurelie, Aurelius, 274

Avantage, at his avantage, in a position where he has the superiority, 64

Avaunt, *n.* boast, 868

Aventure, *n.* fortune, 232; happening, 775; *pl.* happenings, 2; **of aventure,** by chance, 793

Avyseth (yow), *imp.* consider, 612

Awaiteth (on), 3 *s.pr.* watches (for), 591

Ay, *adv.* ever, 404

Baar, *see* **Bere**
Bake, *adj.* baked, *GP* 343
Bank, *n.* coast, 141
Barbarie, Barbary, barbarian lands, 744
Bare, *adj.* unadorned, 12; scantily clad, 872
Barge, *n.* vessel, 142
Bee(n), *v.* be, 56, 636; **Be,** 3 *s.pr. subj.* 123; **Been,** 3 *pl.pr.* are, 18; **Were,** 3 *s.pt. subj.* would be, 147
Beest, *n.* beast, 166
Berd, *n.* beard, 544
Bere, *v.* Baar, 3 *s.pt.* bore, 401; **beren witnesse,** bear witness, 659
Beste, as for the beste, as the best thing to do, 509
Bet, *adj.comp.* better, 714
Beteth, 3 *s.pr.* beats, 58
Bifoore, *adv.* before, 885
Biforn, *prep.* before, 218
Bigan, 3 *s.pt.* began, 222; **Bigonne,** 3 *pl.pt.* began, 307
Bigon, me is wo bigon, *see* **Wo**
Bihe(e)ste, *n.* promise, 455, 833
Bihight, 3 *s.pt.* promised, 80; **Bihighte,** 1 *s.pt.* 851; **Bihighten,** 2 *pl.pt.* 619
Biholde, *v.* look, 155
Bihoveth me, 3 *s.pr.impers.* it is necessary for me, 651
Bileve, *n.* creed, 425
Biloved, *adj.* beloved, 238
Bilyea, Bilia, 747
Birafte, 3 *s.pt.* **birafte hirself hir lyf,** took away her own life, 692
Biseche, 1 *s.pr.* beseech, 9
Bisily, *adv.* assiduously, 343
Bisyde, *adv.* by his side, 533; **ther bisyde,** near there, 194

Bisynesse, *n.* diligence, 119
Bittre, *adj.* bitter, 148
Bitwix(e), *prep.* between, 48, 824
Bityde, *v.* happen, 293
Biwreye, *v.* reveal, 246
Blake, *adj.* black, 160
Blede, *v.* bleed, 486
Blisful, *adj.* joyful, 98; blessed, 337
Blisse, *n.* happiness, 36
Bond, *n.* covenant, 826
Boot, *n.* boat, 286
Borwe, n. to borwe, as a pledge, 526
Bown, *adj.* prepared, 795
Brast, *see* **Breste**
Brawen, *n.* flesh, 546
Breed, *n.* bread, *GP* 341
Breem, *n.* bream, carp, *GP* 350
Breeth, *n.* breath, 774
Breke, *v.* break, 811
Brest, *n.* **under his brest,** within his breast, 401
Breste, 3 *s.pr.subj.* break, 51; **brast anon to wepe,** straightway burst out weeping, 772
Brestyng, *n.* breaking, 265
Breyde, 3 *s.pt.* **out of his wit he breyde,** he went out of his mind, 319
Britayne, Briteyne, Brittany, 21; Britain, 102
Britouns, Bretons, 1
Brutus, Marcus Brutus, 741
Bryd, *n.* bird, 166
Bryngen, *v.* bring, 551
Brynke, *n.* edge, 150; shore, 452
Bugle-horn, *n.* drinking-horn *made from the horn of the 'bugle', or wild ox,* 545
Burel, *adj.* plain, homely, 8
Burned, *adj.* burnished, 539
But, *conj.* unless, 95; only, 167; **but if,** if . . . not, 770

Glossary

Cam, *see* **Come(n)**

Cartage, Carthage, 692

Cas, *n.* matter, 118; situation, 722; case, 806; affair, 842

Castel, *n.* castle, 139

Caughte, 3 *s.pt.* **caughte of this greet routhe,** conceived great pity for this, 812; **swich a pitee caught of,** conceived such pity for, cf. Fr. *prendre pitié,* 32

Causelees, *adv.* without cause, 117

Causes, *n.pl.* reasons, 179

Cedasus, Scedasus, 720

Centris, *n.pl.* centres, 569. *See Appendix IV*

Certein, *adj.* sure, 158

Certes, *adv.* for certain, 609; certainly, 880

Certeyn, *adv.* as a matter of fact, 11

Chalange, 1 *s.pr.* claim, 616

Chaunce, God yeve thee good chaunce, God's blessing upon you, *L* 679

Chaungynge, *n.* **chaungynge of complexioun,** changes in the bodily constitution, 74. *See Notes, GP* 333

Cheere, Chiere, *n.* countenance, 601; **glad chiere,** cheerful expression, 759; **maketh hire good cheere,** entertains her, 390; **dooth chiere and reverence,** gives entertainment and show of respect, 549

Chees, *see* **Chese**

Cherisseth, 3 *s.pr.* cherishes, 846

Cherlyssh, *adj.* mean, ungracious, 815

Ches, *n.* chess, 192

Chese, *v.* choose, 651; **chese**

he, let him choose, 378; **Chees,** 3 *s.pt.* chose, 676

Cheyne, *n.* chain, 648

Chiere, *see* **Cheere**

Chiertee, *n.* love, 173

Citee, *n.* city, 463

Clene, *adj.* clear, 287

Cleped, *pp.* called, 100; **Ycleped,** *pp.* 230

Clerk, *n.* scholar, magician, 449

Cofre, *n.* coffer, chest, 863

Colde, *adj.* gloomy, 156

Colde, *v.* grow cold, 315

Collect, *adj.* **collect yeeris,** tables of the motions of a planet for round periods, 567. *See Appendix IV*

Colours, *n. pl.* ornaments of style (*a rhetorical term*), 15; colours, 16

Come(n), *v.* come, 436, 452; **Comth,** 3 *s.pr.* 57; **Cam,** 3 *s.pt.* 752; **Coome,** 3 *pl.pt.* 304; **Comen,** *pp.* 458

Compaignye, *n.* company, 674; **in compaignye,** in the society of others, 135; **holden compaignye,** keep company, 55

Complayne, *v.* lament, 283

Compleint, *n.* lament, 212

Complexioun, *n.* bodily constitution, balance of humours, 74. *See Notes, GP* 333

Compleynyng, *n.* lament, 23

Comune, *v.* commune, *L* 693

Conclusioun, *n.* summing up, 181; result of the discussion, 306; practical experiment, 555

Confort, *n.* encouragement, 459; **doon confort,** give consolation, 118

Conforten, 3 *pl.pr.* comfort, 115

Constellacioun, *n.* configuration, 73

144

Glossary

Constreyned, *pp.* forced, 56

Contenance, *n.* expression, 777

Continuaunce, sende thee continuaunce, may he grant you perseverance, *L* 680

Contrarien, *v.* oppose, *L* 705

Contree, *n.* country, 92

Convenientz, *see* **Proporcioneles**

Coome, *see* **Come(n)**

Coost, *n.* coast, 287

Coppe, *n.* cup, 234

Corrected, *pp.* corrected, *probably means* adapted to a given locality, 566

Cost, *n.* outlay, expenditure, 849

Countour, *n.* auditor of county finances, *or possibly* pleader in court, *GP* 359

Cours, *n.* course, 143

Covenant, *n.* **holden covenant unto,** kept the agreement with, 879

Craft, *n.* art, trade, 419; skill, 201

Crie (upon), 2 *pl.pr.subj.* cry (over), 788

Cropen, *pp.* **cropen out of the ground,** made your first appearance, 906

Curious, *adj.* occult, 412

Curiously, *adv.* skilfully, elaborately, 201

Cursednesse, *n.* act of wickedness, 564; wickedness, 660

Curteisye, *n.* courtesy, 861

Dar, 1 *s.pr.* dare, 53; **Dorste,** 3 *s.pt.* 28

Daunce, *v.* dance, 665

Dawes, *n.pl.* days, 472

Dayes, *n.pl.* days of respite, 867

Dayesye, *n.* daisy, *GP* 331

Declinacioun, *n.* declination,

altitude, 325, 538. *See Appendix IV*

Dede, Deed, *adj.* dead, 473 628

Dedly, *adj.* dying, 332

Deere, *adj.* dear, 602

Dees, *see* **Pleye(n)**

De(e)th, *n.* death, 314, 655

Defaute, *n.* fault, 82

Defoulen, *v.* defile, 710

Degree, *n.* status (as a husband), 44

Delit, *n.* pleasure, 664

Delitables, *adj.pl.* delightful, 191

Delphos, Delphi, 369

Demeth, *imp.* judge, 790; **demen harm,** suspect evil, 778

Demociones, Demotion's, 718

Departe, 1 *s.pr.subj.* break up, 824

Derke, *adj.* dark, gloomy, 136

Descended, *pp.* alighted, 534

Desdeyn, haveth me nat in desdeyn, do not take offence at me, *L* 700

Despende, *v.* waste, *L* 690

Despeyred, Dispeyred, *pp.* desperate, 235, 376

Despit, *n.* indignation, 663

Destreyneth, 3 *s.pr.* rends, torments, 112

Deth, *see* **Deeth**

Dette, *n.* debt, 870

Devyse, *v.* set forth in detail, 335

Deye, *v.* die, 270; **Dye,** 243, **Dyen,** 732; **Deyde,** 3 *pl.pt.* 721

Deyntee, *n.* pleasure, 295; delight, *L* 681; *pl.* delicacies, *GP* 346

Dianes, Diana's, 682

Diligence, *n.* **doon his diligence,** do his utmost, 550

145

Glossary

Dirke, *adj.* dark, 366
Disconfort, *n.* distress, 188
Discrecioun, *n.* discrimination, *L* 685
Discryve, *v.* describe, 223
Disese, *n.* sorrow, 606
Disport, *n.* recreation, 187
Disporte (hire), *v.* divert (herself), 141
Disputisoun, *n.* disputation, argument, 182
Diverse, *adj.pl.* various, 2
Doghter, *n.* daughter, 718; *pl.* **Doghtren,** 721; **Doghtres,** 662
Doom, *n.* **to my doom,** in my judgment, 220
Doon, *v.* practise, 673; **Dooth,** 3 *s.pr.* does, 72; **Doon,** 3 *pl.pr.* 62; **Dooth,** *imp.* 627; **Do,** *pp.* 625. *As causal auxiliary:* **do me deye,** make me die, 270; **do myn herte breste,** let my heart break, 348; **dide hym swich plesaunce,** gave him such pleasure, 491. *See* **Confort, Chiere, Diligence**
Dormant, *adj.* permanent, *GP* 353
Dorste, *see* **Dar**
Doun (of), *adv.* down (from), 475
Doute, *n.* fear, 388
Drede, *n.* **for drede,** because of fear, 28; **in drede,** in fear, 678; **it is no drede,** there is no doubt, 904; **withouten drede,** certainly, 15
Drede, 1 *s.pr.* fear, 604
Dredful, *adj.* fearful, 601
Dreynte, 3 *pl.pt.* drowned, 670
Drope, *n.* drop, 632
Drough (unto), 3 *s.pt.* drew (towards), 257

Dryve (awey), *v.* drive away, 136; **Dryve,** *pp.* completed, 522
Duren, *v.* continue, 128
Dyen, *see* **Deye**

Ech, *pron.* each, 326
Eek, Eke, *adv.* also, 27, 672
Eft, *adv.* later, 845
Eighe, *n.* eye, 328; **Eyen,** *pl.* 150
Eke, *see* **Eek**
Ekko, Echo, 243
Elles, *adv.* otherwise, 69; else, 189
Emperisse, *n.* empress, 340
Emprented, *pp.* imprinted, 123
Emprentyng, *n.* imprinting, impression, 126
Emprise, *n.* undertaking, 24
Endelong, *prep.* all along, 284
Endyte, *v.* write, relate, 842
Engelond, England, 102
Enquere, *v.* **leete enquere,** had searched for, 671
Ensamples, *n.pl.* examples, 711
Entende (to), *v.* apply himself (to), *L* 689; **Entendeth (to),** 3 *s.pr.* pays attention (to), 389
Entente, *n.* meaning, 251; plan, 470; will, 675; purpose, 784; attention, 801
Envyned, *adj.* stocked with wine, *GP* 342
Equacions, *n.pl.* equations, *corrections, allowances for minor motions,* 571. *See Appendix IV*
Er, *conj.* before, 25
Erst, *adv.* before, 273
Ese, *n.* ease, 80; comfort, 96
Eterne, *adj.* eternal, 157
Evene, *adv.* uniformly, 361
Everych, *pron.* **Everych oother,** each other, 54; **Evericho(o)n,** everyone, 121, 451

146

Glossary

Everydeel, every bit, 580

Excused (of), *pp.* excused (for), 10

Expans, *adj.* **expans yeeris,** tables of the motions of a planet for short periods, 567. *See* **Collect** *and Appendix IV*

Face, *n.* face *(astronomical term denoting the third part of a sign of the zodiac),* 580. *See Appendix IV*

Fader, *n.* father, 681; **Fadres,** *gen.s.* 665

Fadme, *n.* **fyve fadme,** five fathoms, 352

Failled (of), 1 *s.pt.* failed (in), 869

Fallen, *see* **Hand**

Fals, *adj.* false, 654; **fals of,** false in, 889

Fantasye, *n.* imagining, 136

Fare, 1 *s.pr.* get on, 871; **fare amys,** go astray, 590; **beste farynge,** handsomest, 224; **Fare,** *pp.* gone, 461

Faste, *adv.* close, 139

Fasteth, 3 *s.pr.* goes without food, 111

Fauconers, *n.pl.* falconers, 488

Fay, by my fay, by my faith, 766

Feeleth, 3 *s.pr.* **feeleth noght of,** is unaffected by, 19

Feendly ,*adj.* fiendish, 160

Feere, *n.* fear, 152; **for the feere,** for fear, 185

Feestes, *n.pl.* feasts, 434; **at feste,** at a feast, 661

Feith, *n.* promise, 526; **in feith,** in truth, *L* 673

Felawe, *n.* companion, 417; associate, 445

Felicitee, *n.* happiness, *GP* 338

Fer, *adv.* far, 93

Ferther, *adv.* farther, 469

Feste, *see* **Feestes**

Fil, 3 *s.pt.* fell, 594; **fil of his accord,** came to an agreement with him, 33; **fille in speche,** fell into conversation, 256; **fil adoun,** fell down, 372; **hym fil in remembraunce,** it came into his memory, 409; **fille they in tretee,** they fell to bargaining, began negotiating, 511

Fir, Fyr, *n.* fire, 342, 544

Firste, *adj.* original, 3

Fixe, *adj.* fixed, 574

Flour, *n.* flower, 324; **Floures,** *pl.* 200

Folies, *n.pl.* foolish ideas, 294

Folwe, *v.* follow, 41

Foot(e), *n.* step, 395, 469

For, *prep.* at, 68; out of your regard for, 613; for fear of, 724; **for me,** as far as I am concerned, 378

Forbede, 1 *s.pr.* forbid, 773

Fordo, *pp.* ruined, 854

Forlorn, *pp.* lost, 849

Forme, *n.* appearance, 453

Forth, *adv.* continually, 256; onwards 598; **forth right,** straight forward, direct, 795

Forthward, *adv.* forwards, 461

Franchise, *n.* generosity, 816

Frankeleyn, *n.* Franklin, *GP* 331

Fre, *adj.* generous, 914

Freendes, *n.pl.* lovers, 54

Freendly, *adj.* friendly, 759

Frely, *adv.* generously, 896

Fresshe, *adj.* bold, vigorous, 384; brightly coloured, 205

Fressher, *adj.* more lively, 219

Fro, *prep.* from, 93

Ful, *adv.* very, 45; fully, 522

Fulfille, *v.* satisfy, 664

Furye, *n.* Fury, 242 (*see Notes*)

Furyus, *adj.* raging, cruel, 393

Galathee, Galatea, 402

Gan, 3 *s.pt.* began, 127; proceeded to, 754; **Gonne,** 3 *pl.pt.,* 210. *As auxiliary to indicate: past time,* 81; *aspect,* 271. *See Appendix II*

Gardyn-ward, to the gardynward, on his way to the garden, 797

Gawle, Gaul, 703

Geere, *n.* implements, *GP* 352; **Geeris,** *pl.* paraphernalia, 568

Gentil, *adj.* worthy, 1; generous, magnanimous, 835; well-bred, *L* 693

Gentillesse, *n.* courtesy, 46; generosity of mind, magnanimity, 816; manners of high breeding, *L* 694

Gentilly, *adv.* generously, 900; with the sensibility of good breeding, *L* 674

Gerdoun, *n.* reward, 265

Gerounde, Gironde, *a river near Bordeaux,* 514

Gesse, *v.* suppose, 778

Gete, *v.* get, 858

Gilt, *n.* responsibility, 49; guilt, 331

Giltlees, *adj.* guiltless, 610

Gipser, *n.* pouch, *GP* 357

Girdel, *n.* **at his girdel,** from his belt, *GP* 358

Glade, *v.* gladden, 260

Glyde, *v.* flow, 707

Gon, Goon, *v.* go, 395, 101; act, 517; walk, 639; **Goth,** 3 *s.pr.* 638; **Go(o)n,** *pp.* 58, 643; **Go we,** *imp.* let us go, 509; **Gooth**

forth, *imp.* 780; **so moot I goon,** as I hope to live, 69. *See* **A-begged**

Gonne, *see* **Gan**

Governaunce, *n.* government, control, 158; **kan on governaunce,** is capable of self-control, 78

Grace, *n.* mercy, 250; unmerited favour, 617; **bettre grace,** more mercy, 858

Graunte, *v.* consent, 282; allow, 867

Graven, *v.* engrave, 122; **Grave,** *pp.* buried, 268

Grece, Greece, 736

Greet, Grete, *adj.* great, 24, 127; **Gretteste,** *sup.* greatest, 484

Grene, *n.* grass, 154; vegetation, 543

Grette, 3 *s.pt.* greeted, 466

Grevaunce, *n.* distress, 233

Greve, *v.* harm, 426

Grisly, *adj.* horrible, 151

Habradate, Abradates, 706

Halke, *n.* **halke and every herne,** nook and every cranny, 413

Han, *v.* have, 206; **Han,** 3 *pl.pr.* 35; **Hastow,** 2 *s.pr.* hast thou, 881; **Hadde,** 3 *s.pt.* 231; **Hadden,** 3 *pl.pt.subj.* 687

Hand, Hond, *n.* **in myn hand,** your hand on mine, 620; **into youre hond,** into your own keeping, 825; **fallen in myn hond,** passed into my possession, *L* 684

Happe, *v.* befall, 634; **Happed,** 3 *s.pt.* happened, 793

Harm, *see* **Demeth**

Hasdrubales, Hasdrubal's, 691

Glossary

Hastily, *adv.* quickly, 131

Haukes, *n.pl.* hawks, 489

Heed, *n.* head, *GP* 332; beginning, 574

Heele, *n.* prosperity, well-being, 379

Heeng, 3 *pl.pt.* hung, *GP* 358

Heepe, *n.* large number, 785

Heer(e), *adv.* here, 21; **have heer,** here is, 51; **heerof,** of this, 711; **as heer biforn,** before this, formerly, 827

Heere, *v.* hear, 20; **Herde,** 3 *s.pt.* heard, 299; **Herd,** *pp.* 790

Heet, *see* **Highte**

Heigh(e), *adj.* noble, 27; high, 281; great, 815; *see* **An**; **hornes hye,** tall antlers, 483; **Hyeste,** *sup.* highest, 353

Hem, 3 *pl.pers.pron.* them, 5. **Hemself, Hemselven,** 3 *pl. reflex.* themselves, 702, 670

Hente, 3 *s.pt.* seized, 683

Herberwe, *n.* lodging, position (in the ecliptic), 327

Here, *see* **Hire**

Herkneth, *imp.* listen to, 788

Herne, *n. see* **Halke**

Heroun, *n.* heron, 489

Herte, *n.* **til that myn herte breste,** until I die, 51; **hertes lyf,** own dear life, 108

Hertes, *n.pl.* harts, 483

Heste, *n.* promise, 356

Hethen, *adj.* heathen, 585

Hevene, *n.* heaven, 316

Hevy, *adj.* sorrowful, 114

Hevynesse, *n.* sorrow, 120

Hewe, *n.* hue, 308

Hewed, *pp.* coloured, 537

Highte, 3 *s.pt.* was called, 791; **Hight,** *pp.* promised, 615; **Heet,** *pt.* was called, 680

Hir(e), *poss. adj.* their, 1; her, 108, 658

Hire, 3 *s.pers.pron.f.,* to her, 37; **Here,** her, 82; **Hirself, Hirselven,** *reflex.* herself, 644, 689

Holde(n), *v.* hold, 316; keep, 455; consider, 786; **Holde(n),** *pp.* held, 226, 598. *See* **Compaignye**

Holpen, *pp.* helped, 336

Hond, *see* **Hand**

Honured, *pp.* honoured, 744

Hool, *adj.* unwounded, 403; whole, 742

Ho(o)m, *adv.* homewards, 92, 147; home, 130

Hoote, *adj.* hot, 538

Houndes, *n.pl.* dogs, 485

Humble, *adj.* meek, 83

Humblesse, *n.* meekness, 45

Hye, *see* **Heigh(e)**

Illusiouns, *n.pt.* deceptive appearances, 584; **maken illusioun,** cause deception, 556.

Inpossible, *adj.* impossible, 841; *n.* impossibility, 301

Ire, *n.* anger, 73

Jalousie, *n.* jealousy, 40

Janus, *the two-faced God, who gave his name to the first month of the year, January,* 544

Japes, *n.pl.* tricks, 563

Jogelrye, *n.* conjuring, 557

Jolyer, *adj.comp.* more gay, 219

Joye, *n.* joy, 311

Jupartie, *n.* jeopardy, danger, 787

Justeth, 3 *s.pr.* jousts, 390

Kalkuled, *pp.* calculated, 576

Kan, 1 *s.pr.* understand, 558; **Koude,** 3 *s.pt.* could, 95;

Glossary

Kan—*contd.*
  as I kan, in al that evere I kan, as I best kan, to the best of my ability, 7, 290, 604; **kan on,** is wise in, 78

Kayrrud, Kerru, 100 (*see Note*)

Kene, *adj.* sharp, 404

Kepe, *v.* keep, 770; **Kepe,** 3 *s.pr.subj.* may (God) preserve, 181

Kirtel, *n.* tunic, 872

Kithe, *v.* show, 40

Knowe, *pp.* known, 472

Knowes, *n.pl.* knees, 317

Knyt, *pp.* wed, 278; agreed, 522

Koude, *see* **Kan**

Kynde, *n.* **of kynde,** by nature, 60

Kynrede, *n.* kindred, 27

Lacedomye, Lacedaemonia, 672

Lady, *n.* wife, 88; mistress, 89

Lakked, 3 *s.pt.impers.* was lacking, 478

Langour, *n.* languishing, sickness, 393

Langwissheth, 3 *s.pr.* endures pain, 242

Laodomya, Laodamia, 737

Large, *adj.* free, 47

Lasse, *adj.* less, 516

Lat, *see* **Lete**

Latoun, *n. a compound metal containing chiefly copper and zinc;* **hewed lyk latoun,** like copper in colour, 537

Layes, *n.* lays, *short narrative poems,* 2 (*see Notes*); songs, 239

Ledest, 2 *s.pr.* govern, 158; **Leden,** 3 *pl.pr.* lead, conduct, 190; **lede hir lyves,** lead their lives, 36

Le(e)ste, *see* **Atte**

Leeve, *adj.* dear, 899

Lenger, *adj.comp.* longer, 457; *adv.comp.* 842; **ever lenger the moore,** always more and more, 754

Leoun, *n.* Leo (*sign of zodiac*), 350; lion, 438

Lerne, *v.* learn, 70

Lese, *v.* lose, 652

Leste, 3 *s.pr.impers.* it pleases, 177; 3 *s.pt.impers.* it pleased, 527. *See* **List**

Lete, *v.* let, 216; 1 *s.pr.* leave, 182; **Lat,** *imp.* let, 294; **Leet,** 3 *s.pt. used as causal auxiliary,* 707; **leete enquere and seeke,** had enquiries and searches made, 671

Lette, 3 *pl.pr.subj.* hinder, 286

Lettres, *n.pl.* letters, 130

Leve, *n.* leave, 631

Leve, *v.* leave off, 120; **Ylaft,** *pp.* left, 420.

Levere, *adj.* **have I levere to,** will I rather, 652; **I hadde wel levere,** I had much rather, 768; **were hym levere,** he had rather, 814; **I have wel levere,** I will much rather, 823

Leves, *n.pl.* leaves, 200

Lewed, *adj.* stupid, 786

Leyser, *n.* opportunity, 269

Libertee, *n.* liberty, 60

Lighte, *adj.* joyous, 206

Lighte (a)doun, 3 *s.pt.* alighted, 475, 540

Lightned, *pp.* illumined, 342

Liketh, 3 *s.pr.impers.* it pleases, 110; **hym lyked,** it pleased him, 442

Lisse, *n.* relief, 530

Lissed, *pp.* relieved, 462

List, 3 *s.pr.impers.* it pleases, 20; **hem liste,** it pleases them,

143; **listeth nat,** *pers.* does not desire, *L* 689. *See* **Leste**

Lond, *n.* land, *L* 683

Longen, 3 *pl.pr.* belong, 423

Looke (upon), *v.* look (at), 271; **Looketh,** *imp.* take heed, 524; **looke who that,** whoever, 63; **looke what day,** whatever day, 284

Looth, *adj.* **so looth hym was,** so hateful it was to him, 811; **lothest were,** it would be most hateful, 605

Lordshipe, *n.* lordship, rule, 35

Lordynges, *n.pl.* gentlemen, 913

Lorn, *pp.* lost, 329

Lothest, *see* **Looth**

Love, *n.* lover, 214

Lowe, *adv.* **lowe or heighe,** to a low point or high, 327

Luce, *n.* pike, *GP* 350

Lucina, *another name for Diana,* 337

Lucresse, Lucretia, 697

Luna, Moon, 337

Lust, *n.* pleasure, 104; desire, 814

Lusty, *adj.* pleasant, 229; valiant, 383; jovial, 547

Lye, *v.* tell lies, 862

Lye, *v.* lie, 377; **Lith,** 3 *s.pr.* **in yow lith al,** all rests in you, all is in your power, 629

Lyf, *n.* life, 108; **on lyve,** alive, 224

Lyk (to), *adj.* like, 172

Lykerous, *adj.* eager, 411

Lym, *n.* lime, 441

Lyve, *see* **Lyf**

Lyven, *v.* live, 700

Macidonye, Macedonia, 727

Magyk natureel, natural magic, 447

Maister, *n.* master, expert, 494; **Maistres,** *gen.* 512

Maistrie, Maistrye, *n.* domination, 39, 56; **ne sholde upon hym take no maistrie,** would not assume domination for himself, 39

Make(n), *v.* cause, 448, 556; perform, 563; produce, 432; **Maked, Maad,** *pp.* 206, 287; **Maked,** 3 *s.pt.* made, 292; **Maden,** 3 *pl.pt.* composed, 2

Manere, *n.* way, 245; **maner place,** kind of place, 799

Mansioun, *n.* mansion, 577 (*see Notes*)

Mateere, Mater, *n.* things, 19; theme, 239

May, 3 *s.pr.* can, 128; **if I may,** if I can help it, 710

Mayde(n), *n.* maiden, 657, 680

Maydenhede, *n.* virginity, 668

Mecene, Messene, 671

Mede, *n.* meadow, 16

Meenes, *n.pl.* means, instruments, 175

Meke, *adj.* humble, 31

Melesie, Miletus, 701

Mente, 2 *s.pt.* purposed, 273

Merciable, *adj.* merciful, 328

Merk, *n.* image, likeness, 172

Merveille, *n.* marvel, 636

Merveillous, *adj.* marvellous, 498

Meschaunces, *n.pl.* accursed customs, 584; **God yeve hem myschaunce!** May God confound them! 666

Mete, *n.* dinner, *GP* 343; food, *GP* 345

Mirour, *n.* mirror, pattern, 746

Mo, *adj.* more, 704. *See* **Nevere**

Glossary

Monstre, *n.* unnatural thing, 636

Moone, *n.* moan, 212

Moore, *adj.comp.* greater, 346; *adv.comp.* any more, 886; **the moore,** to a greater extent, 36; **the mooste,** *adv.sup.* most, 914

Moorneth, 3 *s.pr.* yearns, 111

Mooste, *see* **Moore**

Moot, 3 *s.pr.* must, 12; **Moot(e),** 3 *pl.pr.* 54, 510; **Moste,** 3 *s.pt.* 215

Morne, *adj.* morning, GP 358

Morwe, *n.* morning, 198; **morwe tyde,** morning time, 193; **by the morwe,** in the morning, GP 334

Muchel, *adv.* much, 421

Muwe, *n.* coop, cage, GP 349

Myn, *poss. adj. before h,* my, 51; **Myselven,** *reflex.pron.* 654

Mynde, *n.* **in mynde,** in the memory, 170

Myschaunce, *see* **Meschaunces**

Name, *n.* title, 43; reputation, 654

Namely, *adv.* especially, 31

Namoore, *adv.* no more, 758; *pron.* 848

Nas, *see* **Nys**

Nat, *adv.* not, 56

Nathelees, *adv.* nevertheless, 215

Ne, *adv.* not, 213

Necligence, *n.* negligence, 524

Nedes, *adv.* needs, necessarily, 455

Nedeth, 3 *s.pr.impers.* **it nedeth nat,** there is no need, 758

Nevere mo, *adv.* never, 368

Newe, *adv.* anew, 307

Nicerates, Niceratus's, 729

Nichanore, Nicanor, 724

Noght, *adv.* not at all, 389; *n.* nought, 909

Nolde, 3 *s.pt.* would not, 784

Noon, *pron.* none, L 677; **or noon,** or no, 70

Nothyng, *adv.* not at all, 938

Nowel, *exclam. a shout of joy,* 547

Ny, *adv.* **wel ny,** very nearly, 528

Nys, 3 *s.pr.* is not, 166; **Nas,** 3 *s.pt.* was not, 632; **Nere (it),** 3 *s.pt.subj.* were (it) not, 606

Nyste, 3 *s.pt.* did not know, 320

O, Oon, *adj.* one, 53; *num.* 6; **many oon,** many a one, 304; **oon the faireste,** one of the fairest, 26. *See* **Oon**

Obeye, *v.* submit to, 54

Obeysaunce, *n.* submission, 31

Observaunces, *n.pl.* customary rites, 248, 583

Of, *prep.* for, 10; about, 2, 106; with, 35; from, 685; by, 699; in, L 678

Ofte tyme, *adv.* often, GP 356

Oght, *indef.pron.* anything, 761

Oghte, 3 *s.pr.* ought, 689

O(o)ld, *adj.* old, 445, 537; *pl.* **olde,** of old, 1

Omer, Homer, 735

On, *prep.* in, 492

Oon, after oon, according to one standard, i.e. uniformly good, GP 341

Oonly, *adv.* alone, 650

Oother, *adj.* other, 196

Operacioun, *n.* experiment, 582; *pl.* working, 421

Opposicioun, *n.* opposition (*An astronomical term for the relation of two planets when they are 180° apart*), 349

Oppresse, *v.* rape, 703

Glossary

Ordinaunce, *n.* arrangements, 195

Orisonte, *n.* horizon, 309

Orisoun, *n.* prayer, 318

Orliens, Orleans, 410

Oute, *adv.* away, 387

Outher, *conj.* either, 49

Oversprynge, 3 *s.pr.subj.* might rise above, 352

Owene, *adj.* own, 172

Pacience, *n.* sufferance, 65

Pacient, *adj.* long-suffering, 63

Paraventure, *adv.* perhaps, 247

Parcel, *n.* part, 144

Pardee, *lit.* 'by God'. *A common oath or asseveration,* indeed, 737

Parfit, *adj.* perfect, 163

Particuler, *adj.* out of the way, 414

Passynge, *pr.p.* surpassing, 221

Payne, *see* **Peyne**

Pedmark, Penmarc'h, 93

Peere, *n.* equal, *L* 678

Penalopee, Penelope, 735

Penaunce, *n.* suffering, 32

Pernaso, Parnassus, *a favourite haunt of the Muses,* 13

Peyne, *n.* pain, sorrow, 29; **up peyne of deeth,** upon pain of death, 773; **dide his payne,** took trouble, tried, 22

Peynte, 3 *pl.pr.* paint, 17

Phebus, the Sun, 537

Phidoun, Phidon, 661

Pitee (of), *n.* pity (for), 32; **is ful greet pitee,** is a very great pity, 720

Pitous, *adj.* sorrowful, 186

Pitously, *adv.* pitiably, 155

Playn, *n.* field of contest, 490

Plentevous, *adj.* plentiful, *GP* 344

Plesaunce, *n.* enjoyment, 5; delight, 209

Plesen, *v.* please, *L* 707

Pley, *n.* play, 280

Pleye(n), *v.* play, 189; perform, 433; *reflex.* amuse themselves 197; **pleye at dees,** play at dice, *L* 690

Pleyn, *adj.* plain, 12; full, *GP* 337

Pleyne, *v.* complain, 68; lament, 609; **pleyne on,** complain against, 647

Pleynt, *n.* lament, 321

Porcia, Portia, *wife of Marcus Brutus,* 740

Possibilitee, *n.* **by possibilitee,** by any possibility, 635

Poynaunt, *adj.* piquant, *GP* 352

Prechen, 3 *pl.pr.* exhort, 116

Preise, 1 *s.pr.* commend, *L* 674

Preyeth, 3 *s.pr.* entreats, 550; **Preyde,** 3 *pl.pt.* 134

Proces, *n.* process, course, 637; **by proces,** in course of time, gradually, 121

Profre (me), 2 *s.pr.* propose (for me), 47

Proporcioun, *n.* the use of proportion, adjustment, 578

Proporcioneles convenientz, suitable proportional parts, tables of proportional parts (*for computing the motions of planets during fractions of a year*), 570

Prosperitee, *n.* condition of well-being, 91

Protheselaus, Protesilaus, 738

Prys, *n.* excellence, 203; esteem, 226

Pryvely, *adv.* privately, 33; not for all to see, 420; secretly, 669

Pured, *adj.* refined, 852

153

Purveiaunce, *n.* providence, 157; provision of necessaries, 196

Queynte, *adj.* elaborate, ingenious, 18
Quod, 3 *s.pt.* said, 273
Quyk, *adj.* alive, 628
Quyked, *pp.* kindled, 342
Quykkest, *adj.sup.* busiest, 794
Quyt, *adj.* discharged, freed from dilemma, 655; repaid, 870; **thee wel yquit,** performed your part well, *L* 673

Rage, *n.* violent sorrow, 128
Ravyng, *n.* wild, delirious talk, 318
Rede, *adj.* red, 440
Reden, *v.* study, 412; read, 721; **Redden,** 3 *pl.pt.* 5
Redressed, 3 *s.pt.* set right the wrong done to, 728
Redy, *adj.* ready, 502
Reft, *pp.* robbed, 309
Reherce, *v.* repeat, 758
Relesse, 1 *s.pr.* remit, 825
Remembraunce, *n.* **have in remembraunce,** remember, 6
Remembre, 3 *pl.pr.* remind, 535
Remenaunt, *n.* remainder, 578
Remoeven, *v.* remove, 513
Repreve (of), *v.* reproach (for), 829
Resoun, *n.* reason, 125
Respiten (me), *v.* grant a respite (to me), 874
Revel, *n.* merrymaking, 307
Reweth, *imp.* have pity, 266
Reyn, *n.* rain, 542
Reyne, *n.* reign, rule, 47

Right, *adv.* just, 508; straight, 682; altogether, 225
Righte, *adj.* direct, 532; own true, 603
Rigour, *n.* unyielding resistance, 67
Rodogone, Rhodogune, 748
Rokkes, *n.pl.* rocks, 151
Romayn, Roman, 696
Romen (hire), *v.* roam, 135
Rootes, *n.pl.* roots, 568. *See Appendix IV*
Roundels, *n.pl.* rondeaux, 240 (*see Notes*)
Routhe, *n.* pity, 553; pitiful sight, 641; **that were routhe,** that would be a pity, 821
Rude, *adj.* unpolished, 10
Rymeyed, *pp.* composed in rhyme, 3
Ryver, *n.* hawking ground on the bank of a river, 488; **Ryveres,** *pl.* rivers, 190

Saleweth, 3 *s.pr.* salutes, 801; **Salewed,** *pp.* 602
Sangwyn, *adj.* sanguine, *the temperament in which the blood predominates over the other humours, giving a ruddy complexion and a courageous, hopeful, amorous disposition, GP* 333
Sauf, *see* **Vouche sauf**
Saufly, *adv.* safely, 53
Saugh, *see* **Seen**
Save, *prep.* except for, 211
Save, *v.* maintain, 770
Say, *see* **Seen**
Sayn, *see* **Seye**
Sayne, Seine, 514
Scithero, Cicero, 14
Secree, *adv.* secretly, 401
See, *n.* sea, 139
Seen, Sene, *v.* see, 83, 403; **Se,**

Glossary

1 *s.pr.* 146; **Say, Seigh, Saugh,** 3 *s.pt.* saw, 416, 142, 138; **Seyn, Ysene,** *pp.* 484, 288

Seigh, *see* **Seen**

Seillynge, *pr.p.* sailing, 143

Seke, *v.* seek, 103; **leete seke,** had sought, 671

Selve, *adj.* same, 686

Semen, 3 *pl.pr.* seem, 161; **hym semed,** it seemed to him, 315

Serement, *n.* oath, 826 (*see Notes*)

Servage, *n.* subjection, 86

Servant, *n.* servant, *professed lover, devoted to the service of a lady,* 84

Servyce, *n.* devotion, 264

Sesons, *n.pl.* seasons, *GP* 347

Sessiouns, *n.pl.* sessions (*of the Justices of the Peace*) *GP* 355

Seten, 3 *pl.pt.* sat, 500

Sette, 3 *s.pt.* set, 104; **sette at noght,** valued at nothing, 113

Seuretee, *n.* security, 873

Seye, Seyn, Seyen, Sayn, *v.* say, tell, 53, 7, 62, 711; **herd me sayd,** heard told by me, 839

Shal, 3 *s.pr.* must, 42; **Shul,** 2 *pl.pr.* must, 70; **Sholde,** 3 *s.pt.* ought, 512

Shame, *n.* **for shame of,** in order not to bring shame upon, 44

Shame(n), *v.* put to shame, 456, 857

Sheene, *adj.* bright, 337

Shipe, *n.* ship, 142; *pl.* **Shippes,** 452

Shirreve, *n.* sheriff, *GP* 359

Sholde, *see* **Shal**

Shoon, 3 *s.pt.* shone, 539

Shoope (hym), 3 *s.pt.subj.* arranged (for himself), 101; **Shopen,** 3 *pl.pt.* arranged, 189

Shortly, *adv.* to speak briefly, 227

Shoures, *n.pl.* showers, 199

Shove, *pp.* moved onwards, 573

Shul, *see* **Shal**

Sighte, *n.* appearance, 205

Sike, *adj.* sick, 392

Siker, *adj.* sure, 431

Sikerly, *adv.* certainly, 870

Sikes, *n.pl.* sighs, 156

Siketh, 3 *s.pr.* sighs, 109

Siknesse, *n.* illness, 73

Sire, *n.* sir, 46; **Sires,** *pl.* gentlemen, 8

Sith, *conj.* since, 46

Sitte, *v.* sit, 149

Sixte, *num.adj.* sixth, 198

Skipte adoun, 3 *s.pt.* leapt down, 694

Slake, *v.* abate, 133

Slee(n), *v.* slay, 267, 689; **Sle,** 2 *s.pr.* 610; **Slow,** 3 *s.pt.* 707; **Slowe,** 3 *pl.pt.* 722; **Slayn, Yslayn,** *pp.* 132, 657

Slepen, *v.* sleep, 764; **Sleepe,** 1 *s.pr.* sleep, 13

Slitte, *v.* pierce, 552

Slouthe, *n.* sloth, 524

Slyde, *v.* slip away, 216; disappear and be forgotten, 294

Smerte, *n.* smart, pain, 148

Snewed, 3 *s.pt.impers.* snowed, abounded, *GP* 345

Snybbed, *pp.* scolded, *L* 688

So (that), *conj.* provided (that), 260; **so God hym save, as** he hoped for salvation, 515

Sobrely, *adv.* gravely, 877

Socour, *n.* aid, 649

Sodeyn, *adj.* immediate, 302

Softe, *adj.* gentle, 199

Solas, *n.* comfort, 94; pleasure, 311

Som, *adj.* some, 123. *See* **Al**

Glossary

Somme, *pron.* some, 486

Somme, *n.* sum, 512

Somtyme, *adv.* sometimes, 72

Somwhat, *adv.* to a slight extent, 236

Somwher, *adv.* somewhere, 189

Sondry, *adj.* various, *GP* 347

Sone, *n.* son, *GP* 336

Songe, 3 *pl.pt.* sang, 4

Sonken, *pp.* sunken, 184

Sonne, *n.* sun, **under sonne,** on earth, 26

Soor, *adj.* sad, 863

Soore, *adv.* sorely, sadly, 298

Sooth, Sothe, *n.* **sooth seyen, the sothe tellen,** tell the truth, 62, 227

Sope, *n. piece of bread toasted and soaked in spiced wine, GP* 334

Sope(e)r, *n.* supper, 481, 502

Sorwe, *n.* sorrow, 127

Sorweful, *adj.* sorrowful, 300

Soupe, *v.* have supper, 509

Soveraynetee, *n.* supremacy, 43

Sovereyn, *adj.* supreme, 844

Spak, *see* **Speken**

Speche, *n.* speech, 10. *See* **Fil**

Spedde (hym), 3 *s.pt.reflex.* hastened, 554

Speere, *n.* sphere, 572

Speken, *v.* speak, 75; **Spak,** 3 *s.pt.* spoke, 320

Spryng flood, *n.* spring tide, 362

Sprynge, *v.* spring up, 439

Spyed, 3 *s.pt.* spied, 798

Squier, *n.* squire, 218; servant, 501

Stable, *adj.* unchangeable, 163

Stant, 3 *s.pr.* stands, is set, 546

Stille, *adj.* at rest, 500; quiet, 764

Stirte, 3 *s.pt.* **up stirte,** leapt up, 460; **Stirt,** *pp.* leapt, 669

Stoon, *n.* stone, 122

Straunge, *adj.* **made it straunge,** made difficulties about it, 515

Straw for, I do not care a straw for, Fiddlesticks to, *L* 695

Stremes, *n.pl.* beams, 539

Strete, *n.* street, 794

Stryf, *n.* quarrel, 49

Studie, *n.* study, 499

Stuwe, *n.* fishpond, *GP* 350

Stymphalides, Stymphalis, 680

Stynten, *v.* cease to speak of, 106

Subtil, *adj.* expert, 553; **Subtile,** *pl.* 433

Subtilly, *adv.* expertly, 576

Suffrance, *n.* forbearance, 80

Suffre, *v.* endure, 69

Suffyse, *v.* be able, *L* 706

Supersticious, *adj.* pertaining to diabolic art, 564

Surement, *n.* security, 826 (*see Notes*)

Sursanure, *n.* wound healed only on the surface, 405

Sustene (hire), *v.* hold (herself) up, 153

Suster, *n.* sister, 337

Sweete, *n.* beloved, 270

Swerd, *n.* sword, 552

Swere, *v.* swear, 81; **Swoor,** 3 *s.pt.* 37

Swich, *adj.* such, 19; **Swiche,** *pl.* 16

Swowne, *n.* swoon, 372

Swowneth, 3 *s.pr.* swoons, 641

Swyn, *n.* boar, 546

Syn, *conj.* since, 283

Taak, *see* **Take**

Tables, *n.pl.* the game of backgammon, 192 (*see Notes*); **tables Tolletanes,** Toletan astronomical tables, tables pertaining to Toledo, 565

156

Glossary

Take, *pp.* taken, 84; **Taak,** *imp.* 279

Tarie, 2 *pl.pr.subj.* delay, 525

Tarquyn, Tarquinius Sextus, 699

Teere, *n.* tear, 186

Tellen, *v.* tell, 233; **Toold,** 3 *s.pt.* 757

Temperaunce, *n.* self-restraint, 77

Terme, *n.* term, *a division of the sign of the zodiac,* 580. *See Appendix IV.* **Termes,** *pl.* expressions, 558

Thanke (of), *v.* thank (for) 861; **Thonketh,** 3 *s.pr.* thanks, 837

Thanne, *adv.* then, 86

Thennes, *adv.* thence, 252

Ther, *adv.* there, 71; where, 93; **ther as,** where, 796; **therby,** near it, 407; **therinne,** on it, 123; **therto,** in addition, 27; for it, 622; **therwith,** with it, 223

Thider, *adv.* thither, 783

Thilke, *adj.* that same, 180; those same, 585

Thise, *demon.adj.* these, 1

Tho, *adv.* then, 304

Tho(u)gh, *conj.* though, 611; if, *L* 701

Thoght, *n.* thought, care, 114, 376

Thonketh, *see* **Thanke**

Thral, *n.* slave, 61

Thridde, *num.adj.* third, 751

Thriftily, *adv.* politely, 466

Thurgh, *prep.* through, 127

Thyng, *n.* anything, 12; contract, 771

Thynke, *v.* think, 149

Thynketh, 3 *s.pr.impers.* seems, 914; **it thynketh me,** 690; **Thoughte,** 3 *s.pt.* hire

thoughte, it seemed to her, 699

Til, *conj.* until, 123; **til that,** 51; *prep.* to, 900

Tiraunt, *n.* tyrant, 679; **Tirauntz,** *pl.* 660

To, *adv.* too, 18

Tolletanes, *see* **Tables**

Tomorwe, *adv.* tomorrow, 525

Tonge, *n.* language, 3

Touche, *v.* reach, 407

Touchynge, *prep.* concerning, 422

Toun, *n.* town, 693

Trappe, *n.* trap, 633

Travaille, *n.* labour, 909

Tregetours, *n.pl.* conjurers, magicians, 433

Trespas, *n.* **doon trespas,** sin, 658

Tretee, *n.* negotiation, bargaining, 511. *See* **Fil**

Trewe, *adj.* faithful, 50; **Treweste,** *sup.* 831

Trewely, *adv.* truly, 202; faithfully, 523

Troie, Troy, 738

Trouthe, *n.* **have heer my trouthe,** here is my solemn promise, 51; **by my trouthe,** on my word of honour, 523; **My trouthe I plighte,** I give you my word, 829

Turned (hym), 3 *s.pt.* went, 303

Tweye, *num.adj.* two, 587

Tweyne, *num.* two, 48

Tyme, *n.* opportunity, 555; **a tyme,** for a time, 215; **after the tyme,** in accordance with the occasion, 77

Under, *prep.* within, 401

Undertake, 1 *s.pr.* declare, 503

157

Glossary

Unnethe(s), *adv.* scarcely, 28, 639

Unresonable, *adj.* unreasonable, not in accordance with reason, 164

Untrewe, *adj.* unfaithful, 276

Unwar, *adj.* unwary, 648

Unwityng (of), without the knowledge (of), 228

Up, *prep.* **up peyne of deeth,** upon pain of death, 773

Upon, *prep.* in, 217; over, with respect to, 788

Useden, 3 *pl.pt.* practised, 585

Vavasour, *n.* vavasour, *great landholder but below the rank of baron, GP* 360

Venquysseth, 3 *s.pr.* overcomes, puts an end to, 66

Verray, *adj.* excessive, 152; **verray paradys,** Paradise itself, 204

Vertu, *n.* virtue, 65

Vertuous, *adj.* virtuous, accomplished, 225, *L* 687

Vileynye, *n.* **dide hire vileynye,** violated her, 696

Virelayes, *n.pl.* virelays, *a song with a fixed form,* 240 (*see Notes*)

Vitaille, *n.* food, 196

Vouche sauf, *v.* grant, 873; **Voucheth sauf,** *imp.* permit, 335; **Vouche sauf,** 3 *s.pr.subj.* grant, 363; 2 *pl.pres. subj.* condescend, 626

Voyded, *pp.* dismissed, 442; **Yvoyded,** *pp.* removed, 451

Waketh, 3 *s.pr.* lies awake, 111

Wan, 3 *pl.pt.* won, 693

War, *adj.* wary, 833

Warisshed, *pp.* cured, 148

Wax, 3 *s.pt.* grew, 537

Way, *see* **Wey**

Wayleth, 3 *s.pr.* laments, 111; **Wailleth,** 640

Wayten, *v.* lie in wait for, 555

Weel, *see* **Wel**

Weepe, *see* **Wepe**

Wel, *adv.* well, 138; easily, 448; much, 723; *used emphatically in* **wel unnethes,** scarcely, 28; **Weel,** *adv.* perfectly, 579

Welfare, *n.* well-being, 130

Welles, *n.pl.* springs, 190

Wende, 2 *pl.pr.* go, 915; **Wente,** 3 *s.pt.* went, 262; **Wenten,** 3 *pl.pt.* went, 505; **Went,** *pp.* gone, 263

Wene, *v.* imagine, 559; **Wende,** 3 *s.pt.* expected, 633

Wepe, *v.* weep, 772; **Weep,** 3 *s.pt.* wept, 408, 474; **Weepe,** 3 *s.pt.subj.* 753

Were, 3 *s.pt.subj.* might be, 25; should be, 49

Werk, *n.* work, 162; trouble, 'to do', 398; **word ne werk,** word nor deed, 277

Werre, *n.* hostility, 49

Wey, *n.* way, 461; **at the leeste way,** at least, 709

Whan, *conj.* when, 91; **whan so,** whenever, 297

What, *inter.pron.* why, 457; **what for . . . and,** both because of . . . and, 529

Wheither, *conj.* whether, 378

Wher, *conj.* whether, 590; **wher-so,** whether, 70

Where as, *adv.* where, 94

Which, *pron.* who, 212; **the whiche that,** *pron.acc.* whom, 472; **which a wyf,** what kind of wife, 734; **Whiche,** *adj.pl.* 176

Whiderward, *adv.* whither, 802

158

Glossary

Whil, *conj.* while, 498

Whiles, *conj.* whilst, 410

Whit, *adj.* white, *GP* 332

Wight, *n.* man, 71

Wighte, *n.* **of wighte,** by weight, 852

Wirkyng, *n.?* motion, ?calculation, 572

Wise, *adj.* prudent, 79

Wise, Wyse, *n.* manner, way, 23, 336

Wisly, *adv.* **ful wisly,** in very truth, 81; **God so wisly have,** (as I hope) God indeed may have, 767

Wiste, *see* **Woot**

Wit, *n.* understanding, 277; mind, 319; **to my wit,** to my knowledge, 167; *pl.* **Wittes,** intelligence, *L* 706

With, *prep.* to the accompaniment of, 4; by, 267; with, 505

Withal, *adv.* also, *L* 687

Withoute, *adv.* outwardly, 403

Wo, *n.* woe, 29; **wo was,** sad was, 299; **me is wo bigon,** I am oppressed with grief, 608

Wol(e), 1 *s.pr.* will, 50, *L* 703; 3 *pl.pr.* wish, 55; 2 *pl.pr.subj.* wish, 70, 508; **Wolde,** 3 *s.pt.* 152; 1 *s.pt.subj.* should like 913; **Wolden,** 3 *pl.pt.* wished, 673; **ne wolde nevere God . . . were,** may it never be God's will that there should be, 48–9; **God wolde,** would to God, 268; **wolde ye,** if you would, 873

Wonder, *adj.* wonderful, 467

Wondren (on), *v.* wonder (at), 806

Wone, *n.* custom, *GP* 335

Wonne, *pp.* won, 25

Woot, 1 *s.pr.* know, 177; **Woost,** 2 *s.pr. L* 696; **Woot,** 3 *s.pr.* 621; **Wiste,** 3 *s.pt.* knew, 251

Worshipe, *n.* glory, 103; dignity, 254

Worthy, *adj.* distinguished, 505

Worthynesse, *n.* excellence, 30

Wowke, *n.* week 453. *See* **Wyke**

Wrapped, *pp.* involved, entangled, 648

Wrecche, *adj.* wretched, 312

Wrecchednesse, *n.* wretched work, 563; miserable act, 815

Wreken, *pp.* avenged, 76

Wreye, *v.* disclose, 236

Wro(u)ghte, 3 *s.pt.* performed, 25, 494; **Wroght,** *pp.* made, 164

Wyf, *n.* wife, 89; **Wyves,** *pl.* 110

Wyfhod, *n.* wifeliness, 743

Wyfly, *adj.* befitting a wife, 745

Wyke, *n.* week, 587. *See* **Wowke**

Wyl, *n.* desire, 41; will, *L* 704; **with good wyl,** willingly, 7

Wyn, *n.* wine, 74

Wys, *adj.* wise, prudent, 83

Wys, *adv.* **God helpe me so as wys!** so indeed may God help me, 762

Yaf, *see* **Yeve**

Ydel, in ydel, in vain, 159

Ye, *adv.* yes, 764

Ye, 2 *pl.pers.pron.* you, 20; **Yow,** *dat.* 20

Yeer, *n.* year, 98; **two yeer,** two years, 105

Yerd, *n.* garden, 543

Yet, *adv.* notwithstanding, 282; **as yit,** up to now, 869; **yet shal,** shall again, *L* 688

159

Glossary

Yeve, *v.* give, 521; **Yaf,** 3 *s.pt.*
gave, 275; **Yeve,** *pp.* given,
742. *See* **Chaunce, Mys-
chaunce**

Yfostred, *pp.* helped, 166

Yfynde, *v.* find, 445; *pp.*
Yfounde, 562

Yis, *adv.* yes, 659

Yit, *see* **Yet**

Yknowe, *v.* know, discern, 179

Ylaft, *see* **Leve**

Ymaginatyf, *adj.* given to
imagining, suspicious, 386

Ynogh, Ynow, *adj.* enough, 911,
L 708

Yond, *adv.* yonder, 618

Yong, *adj.* young, 225; **Yonge,**
pl. 411

Yoore, of tyme yoore, of
olden time, 255

Yowthe, *n.* youth, *L* 675

Ypayed, *pp.* paid, 910

Yquit, *see* **Quyt**

Ystiked, *pp.* stabbed (to death),
768

Ywis, *adv.* surely, 655